P9-CDB-316

John Muir
Prophet Among the Glaciers

About the Book

An unwearying wanderer, a keen observer, a sensitive and passionate writer. That was John Muir, who went forth year after year into the wilderness to study wildlife, climate, geology. In this perceptive, absorbing biography author Robert Silverberg reveals why Americans today revere Muir's memory as a great leader in the struggle against man's ruination of his own environment. Though Muir was born more than a century and a half ago, Silverberg portrays a man as modern in outlook as today's youth.

LIVES TO REMEMBER

JOHN MUIR

Prophet Among the Glaciers

by Robert Silverberg

G. P. Putnam's Sons

New York

For Paul and Neola
In fond memory of Kings Canyon days and nights

 Published simultaneously in Canada by
Longmans Canada Limited, Toronto.
Library of Congress Catalog Card Number: 74-183391
PRINTED IN THE UNITED STATES OF AMERICA
12 up

Contents

1

Scotland

In Marin County, California, about an hour's drive from San Francisco, there is a splendid grove of giant redwood trees in a canyon near the foot of Mount Tamalpais. The deep-toned chocolate-colored trunks rise clean and straight to heights of hundreds of feet, and often the trees grow close together, so that they seem to form the pillars of some colossal cathedral. There are 510 acres of redwoods in this grove, and no lumberman will ever fell them, for the trees belong to all the people of the United States as a living memorial to a great man. They were given to the government in 1908 by William Kent, a California Congressman, in honor of his friend John Muir. Thousands of Americans come each year to Muir Woods National Monument, as the grove is known, to stand in awe beneath those towering, majestic redwoods.

All across the West the name of John Muir marks the map. Alaska offers Muir Glacier, Muir Inlet, Muir Point, and Mount Muir. There is another Muir Glacier on the slopes of Washington's Mount

Rainier; there is another Mount Muir in Sequoia National Park, California. In Tulare County, California, we find Muir Lake, Muir Grove, and Muir Mountain. Fresno County, California, holds Muir Gorge and Muir Pass. And there are numerous other landmarks bearing John Muir's name, for many communities were eager to pay homage to this beloved and wise man. There was no explorer of natural wonders more tireless than he, and there were few places in the Western realm of spectacular peaks and glaciers and forests that he did not enter.

An unwearying wanderer, a keen observer, a sensitive and passionate writer, Muir went forth year after year into the wilderness to study wildlife, climate, geology, and anything else that caught his interest. Each year he emerged from his forest solitude refreshed and renewed, eager to share what he had learned. He wrote of trees, birds, storms, mountains, forest fires, bears, earthquakes, lakes, valleys, squirrels, wild flowers, waterfalls, and all the other wonders, great and small, of the unspoiled Western mountains, and he told of these things with such marvelously infectious enthusiasm that it is difficult, after reading his prose, to resist rushing out to follow in his path.

But though Muir's accomplishments as a scientist and as a writer were considerable, we revere his memory today chiefly because he was so eloquent a leader of the struggle against man's ruination of his own environment. With the zeal of a Biblical prophet he cried out against those greedy ones who would have destroyed our natural heritage for the sake of a few quick dollars. To protect the remaining wild lands he wrote countless articles, pamphlets, and books; he approached presidents and legislators and asked their support; and he founded an organization, the Sierra Club, that still vigilantly guards the wilderness. John Muir saved much of that wilderness for us, though he went to his grave disappointed that he could not have saved more. We who live in an era of spreading ecological crisis, who find the world turning to ash and smoke about us, owe an immense debt to old John Muir; without him, things would be ever so much worse than they are.

This man who was so deeply concerned with the preservation of the American wilderness was born in Scotland in 1838. His father, Daniel Muir, was a tall, restless man, intense and stern. A sketch of Daniel Muir by his son John declares that he was "a remarkably bright, handsome boy, delighting in athletic games and eager to excel in everything. He was notably fond of music, had a fine voice, and usually took a leading part in the merry song-singing gatherings of the neighborhood. Having no money to buy a violin, when he was anxious to learn to play that instrument, he made one with his own hands, and ran ten miles to a neighboring village through mud and rain after dark to get strings for it."

But at the age of fourteen Daniel Muir underwent a powerful religious experience that would carry him far from games and merry song singing. What he called "the ecstasy of the Apostles" surged through his soul, sweeping him with spiritual emotions so strong that they reshaped his life. He developed a piety that bordered on fanaticism and devoted his whole energy to prayer and to the study of the Bible, in which he believed all truth was to be found. Now he frowned on trivial amusements that tended to interfere with his concentration on holy matters. He sang nothing but hymns; he read nothing but his Bible. He looked with suspicion on anything not immediately religious in content. Later in his life he would bitterly oppose his son John's interest in nature and love for travel, telling him, "You are God's property, soul and body and substance—give those powers up to their owner!"

This rigid-minded, salvation-hungry young man saw no future for himself in Scotland, where poverty was widespread and only the rich could own land. He dreamed of going to America, where an untamed wilderness waited to be exploited, where anyone could have his own farm and live the life he chose. In 1825, when he was twenty-one years old, Daniel went down to the city of Glasgow with no possessions other than his Bible, his fiddle, a few shillings, and the clothes he wore. He hoped to find a job and earn enough money to pay for his passage to the New World; but there were no jobs to be had, and soon he enlisted in the British army for lack of other opportunity.

He took readily to army discipline and became an excellent soldier. The army made him a recruiting sergeant, sending him through Scotland to persuade boys to sign up. His duties brought him in 1829 to Dunbar, in eastern Scotland, where he met a girl who had inherited her father's grain-and-food store. Daniel swiftly married her, obtained his release from military service, and went into business as a merchant. His honesty and industriousness won him many new customers, and soon he was one of the most prosperous men in town.

His wife died suddenly in 1832. Since God had commanded man to be fruitful and multiply, Daniel lost little time in seeking a new bride, and late in 1833 he married Ann Gilrye, a quiet, gray-eyed girl whose family belonged to the town's leading gentry. There was some murmuring in Dunbar about the marriage, for the stern young shopkeeper was thought to be below Ann's social station, and his ferocious religious zeal seemed excessive even to the devout.

She was, John Muir wrote, "conservative, of pious, affectionate character, fond of painting and poetry." But there would be no painting in the Muir household: Daniel informed her that all such "folderol" was forbidden by the Bible, which decrees, "Thou shalt not make unto thee any graven image," and the walls of the house were left bare. Chattering at mealtimes was forbidden; the chief family activity was prayer. But Ann learned to abide by the strict rules of her pious husband.

Children came quickly: Margaret in 1834, Sarah in 1836, John in 1838, David in 1840, Daniel, Junior, in 1843, and twins, Mary and Anna, in 1846. John, the eldest son, was an active, alert child with vivid auburn hair and inquisitive blue eyes. Energetic and boundlessly curious, he scampered and scrambled into every corner of the house and garden. When he was no more than three years old, his grandfather began taking him on long walks down country lanes. These walks were his earliest memories when he wrote the story of his boyhood some seventy years later. Once, he recalled, he and his grandfather were hiking through a hayfield and sat down on a haystack to rest. Young John heard "a sharp, prickly, stinging cry, and, jumping up eagerly, called grandfather's attention to it. He said he heard only the wind, but I insisted on digging into the hay and turning it over until we discovered the source of the strange exciting sound—a mother field mouse with half a dozen naked young hanging to her teats. This to me was a wonderful discovery. No hunter could have been more excited on discovering a bear and her cubs in a wilderness den."

His boyhood was wild and strenuous, full of wrestling, running, snowball fights, and climbing—especially climbing. John was a superb climber, and danger meant nothing to him. He loved crawling up and down sheer walls, clinging to the tiniest handholds and footholds. Thousand-year-old Dunbar Castle, a crumbling ruin, was one place where he particularly loved to climb, though the perils were great. "I was so proud of my skill as a climber," he wrote, "that when I first heard of hell from a servant girl who loved to tell its horrors and warn us that if we did anything wrong we would be cast into it, I always insisted that I could climb out of it. I imagined it was only a sooty pit with stone walls like those of the castle, and I felt sure there must be chinks and cracks in the masonry for fingers and toes."

He had plenty of opportunity to develop abilities as a fighter, too. Warfare was a way of life among the boys of Dunbar. From the age of five or six onward, he passed scarcely a day without a fistfight. To be a good fighter, he later declared, "was our highest ambition, our dearest aim in life in or out of school." Aside from these single combats, Muir and his playmates gathered every Saturday afternoon on a field near the castle where actual battles had been fought since Roman times, and there, choosing sides and arming themselves with sticks and stones, they reenacted the famous military clashes of Scottish history. Though he greatly enjoyed this rough-and-tumble stuff, Muir quickly came to understand how foolish and unnecessary the wars of his ancestors had been. War, he was to write, was "the farthest-reaching and most infernal of all civilized calamities," and in adult life he regarded war as a mere extension of boyhood mischief into the grown-up world. He refused to volunteer for military service at any time and spoke scathingly of how nations "start talking about honor, or something or other, and declare this and so—a boys' war—a big boys' war—no sense in it!"

There was a casual savagery about many of his youthful amusements, and he repented of them in later life. The Dunbar boys diverted themselves with bloody dogfights, used stray cats as targets in rock-throwing contests, and climbed the walls of slaughterhouses to watch in delight as pigs were being butchered. Once, to test the story that cats always land on their feet, Muir and some friends dropped a tomcat from a top-floor window of his house. "I can remember to this day," he wrote, "how the poor creature in danger of his life strained and balanced as he was falling and managed to alight on his feet. This was a cruel thing for even wild boys to do, and we never tried the experiment again, for we sincerely pitied the poor fellow when we saw him creeping slowly away, stunned and frightened, with a swollen black and blue chin."

But there were gentler moments, also, when John went down to the seashore near Dunbar and prowled through the pools in the rocks, spying on their abundant population of eels, crayfish, crabs, clams, and water plants. He took intense pleasure in these investigations and in his hikes through the countryside to collect berries and peer at birds' nests. "How our young wondering eyes," he wrote, "reveled in the sunny, breezy glory of the hills and the sky, every particle of us thrilling and tingling with the bees and glad birds and glad streams! Kings may be blessed; we were glorious, we were free—school cares and scoldings, heart thrashings and flesh thrashings alike, were forgotten in the fullness of Nature's glad wildness. These were my first excursions—the beginnings of lifelong wanderings."

School was a grim business. The teachers were inflexibly strict, and the work was hard. From the age of eight, he wrote, he "had to get three lessons every day in Latin, three in French, and as many in English, besides spelling, history, arithmetic, and geography." Memorization was the main activity: "We were simply driven point-blank against our books like soldiers against the enemy, and sternly ordered 'Up and at 'em. Commit your lessons to memory.' " In class the young scholars were required to recite long lists of rules "over and over again, as if all the regular and irregular incomprehensible verb stuff was poetry." Any mistake, however trivial, brought a whipping from the schoolmaster, "for the grand, simple, all-sufficing Scotch discovery had been made that there was a close connection between the skin and the memory, and that irritating the skin excited the memory to any required degree." Aside from all this, John's father compelled him to devote much of his after-school time to memorizing the Bible, with thrashings again the penalty for any lapses of memory. "By the time I was eleven years old," he said, "I had about three fourths of the Old Testament and all of the New by heart and by sore flesh. I could recite the New Testament from the beginning of Matthew to the end of Revelation without a single stop."

Though these methods of education seem strange and harsh to us, and though they filled John's mind with much that he termed mere "cinders and ashes," he looked back later on his schooldays without resentment. The severe discipline had strengthened and deepened his mind, and his powerful literary style owed much to his early training in grammar and to his intimate knowledge of the King James Version of the Bible. The Latin that had been crammed into him served him well in the scientific studies of his later years.

Nor was all his schoolwork a matter of rules and dull recitations. One of his grammar-school readers contained some natural history sketches that aroused wonder and excitement in him. A piece by the Scottish naturalist Alexander Wilson, who had spent many years exploring the forests of America, offered vivid, magical images of hawks and eagles soaring over that unknown wilderness. Even more memorable was an essay by John James Audubon on the passenger pigeon, a bird that traveled the New World in incredible flocks of many millions, darkening the sky like clouds. To John Muir, who by then had just about exhausted the meager natural history of his native district, America seemed a land of endless miracles.

During the Dunbar years, Daniel Muir too had never ceased to dream of moving to America, even though he was thriving as a merchant in his homeland. But he probably never would have succeeded in uprooting himself if it had not been for his obsession with religion. Unable to find a church that suited him, Daniel had joined one sect after another, until at last he enrolled in a new movement called the Disciples of Christ. Founded by two Scots, Thomas and Alexander Campbell, the Disciples sought to return to the principles of Christianity in its earliest days. Alexander Campbell had emigrated to the United States and had won many followers there; in the 1840's he came back to Scotland to preach his creed to his own people. Daniel Muir quickly was captured by Campbell's fervor and, in 1848, suddenly announced to his startled family that he was going to sell his business so that they all could move to America. There, he said, in the land of religious freedom, the Muirs would settle among a group of Disciples and start life anew as farmers.

His wife's parents so strongly opposed this move that Daniel was forced to alter his plan slightly. Instead of taking everyone with him at once, he would go to the New World with just his sons John and David and his daughter Sarah. The other children—Margaret, Daniel, and the twins—would remain behind in Scotland with their mother until their new home was ready to receive them.

Selling the business took time, though, and as the months passed, John began to doubt that any of this would ever come to pass. Then, on the night of February 18, 1849, Daniel did not return home at the usual time for afternoon tea. John—a few months short of his eleventh birthday—and his brother David went across the street to their grandfather's home to do their evening studying. Abruptly Daniel came in and told them they could forget about their homework that night. The shop had been sold; everything was arranged; they were leaving for America in the morning!

2

A New World

The voyage lasted six weeks and three days. John's father and sister spent most of their time belowdecks, enduring the miseries of seasickness, but John and David had a fine time watching the sailors at work, joining in their songs, learning the names of the ropes and sails, and helping wherever they were permitted. As the ship neared the shores of America, John stared in awe at the dolphins and whales swimming nearby, and watched the swoops and dives of the splendid sea-birds.

As a British subject, Daniel had intended to settle in Canada. But during the journey he heard from some of his fellow immigrants that in Canada "the woods were so close and heavy that a man might wear out his life in getting a few acres cleared of trees and stumps." The land was just as fertile in Wisconsin and Michigan, he was told, and far more easily brought under cultivation. So he decided that the Muirs would make their new home in the United States.

The ship docked in New York City. Daniel and his three children went up the Hudson to Albany and westward across New York State via the Erie Canal to Buffalo. A steamer then took them through the Great Lakes to Milwaukee, where, for $30, Daniel hired a farmer to haul them and all their baggage to a town called Kingston, 100 miles away. A Scot they had met in Buffalo had advised them to go there, saying that other Scots were already settled there.

With the help of his countrymen in Kingston, Daniel rented temporary lodgings and acquired an 80-acre tract of forest 10 miles outside town; the woods were sunny and open, and there was a lake on the property filled with fish. Daniel and a few of his new neighbors set to work at once, chopping down some oaks and building, in a single day, a small one-windowed shanty to hold the family until a more substantial house could be built. One morning in May an oxcart brought the three children and the family belongings out from Kingston to what was to become the Muir farm. "Just as we arrived at the shanty," John wrote, "before we had time to look at it or the scenery about it, David and I jumped down in a hurry off the load of household goods, for we had discovered a blue jay's nest, and in a minute or so we were up the tree beside it, feasting our eyes on the beautiful green eggs and beautiful birds—our first memorable discovery. The handsome birds had not seen Scotch boys before and made a desperate screaming as if we were robbers like themselves; though we left the eggs untouched, feeling that we were already beginning to get rich, and wondering how many more nests we should find in the grand sunny woods. Then we ran along the brow of the hill that the shanty stood on, and down to the meadow, searching the trees and grass tufts and bushes, and soon discovered a bluebird's and a woodpecker's nest, and began an acquaintance with the frogs and snakes and turtles in the creeks and springs. . . . Oh, that glorious Wisconsin wilderness!"

This new world was a wonderland. All about him John saw huge trees, unfamiliar birds and plants, the wonders of an almost untouched woods. "When we first saw Fountain Lake Meadow, on a sultry evening, sprinkled with millions of lightning-bugs throbbing with light, the effect was so strange and beautiful that it seemed far too marvelous to be real," he wrote. An older friend explained the seeming miracle to John and David and caught some of the insects for them; the boys took them to the shanty, "where we watched them throbbing and flashing out their mysterious light at regular intervals, as if each little passionate glow were caused by the beating of a heart."

But after those first few weeks of romping in the woods, of exploring the world of the snipe and the partridge and the frog, came the hard work of making a farm. The process began by using an ox-drawn plow to rip up the underbrush. Then severed roots and stumps had to be pulled up. John and his brother were spared from such heavy labor as this, but they were kept busy piling the debris in heaps and burning it. The newly cleared land then was planted, and when the planting was done, Daniel Muir set about building the family's permanent house. He brought a load of fine white pine back from Milwaukee, hired a few carpenters to help him, and in just a few months put up an imposing eight-room dwelling of two and a half stories. It was finished in October, and early in November Ann Muir arrived from Scotland with Margaret, Danny, and the three-year-old twins. John and David and Sarah had plenty of stories to tell of life in America—stories of the Indians who still lived in that part of Wisconsin, stories of forest adventure, stories of the fun they had had with the pony, Jack, that Daniel had allowed them to have.

The winter's chores were arduous, and the heaviest burdens fell to John, the eldest boy. He rose at six in the morning to feed the horses and cattle, grind axes, bring in firewood, and fetch water from the spring. After breakfast came even harder work: chopping wood into fence rails. "Making rails was hard work and required no little skill," Muir wrote. "I used to cut and split a hundred a day from our short, knotty oak timber, swinging the axe and heavy mallet, often with sore hands, from early morning to night. . . . I rather liked it, for I was proud of my skill, and tried to believe that I was as tough as the timber I mauled, though this and other heavy jobs stopped my growth and earned for me the title 'Runt of the family.' " By ordinary standards John was no runt, for in manhood he reached a height of five feet nine, above average in his time. But the Muirs were a tall family, and to the others he did seem short.

His chores brought him close to the farm animals—to the hardworking oxen, those "wise, patient, plodding animals" that "did all the ploughing, logging, hauling, and hard work of every sort," and to the horses and cattle. Working every day with these creatures, he came to know and love them as friends. "We soon learned," he wrote, "that each ox and cow and calf had individual character." When Daniel Muir caused the death of one of John's favorite horses by driving the poor beast 24 miles over a sandy road in order to get to a prayer meeting on time, John was bitter and resentful. Animals, he was coming to realize, "are our earth-born companions and fellow mortals," and he hated "the mean, blinding, loveless doctrine . . . that animals have neither mind nor soul, have no rights that we are bound to respect, and were made only for man to be petted, spoiled, slaughtered, or enslaved."

In the spring of 1850, when John was twelve, he was put to work guiding the plow, though his head "reached but little above the handles." It was rugged work, since the ground that year was still full of stumps that had to be dodged. The chief crop was wheat, and with the summer came new toil: "Mowing, hoeing, cradling wheat, hauling it to the barns, etc. No rest in the shade of trees on the side of the fields. When tired we dared not even go to the spring for water in the terrible thirst of the muggy dog-days, because the field was in sight of the house and we might be seen." In his autobiography he declares, "We were all made slaves through the vice of over-industry. . . . We were called in the morning at four o'clock and seldom got to bed before nine, making a broiling, seething day seventeen hours long loaded with heavy work. . . . In the harvest dog-days and dog-nights and dog-mornings, when we arose from our clammy beds, our cotton shirts clung to our backs as wet with sweat as the bathing-suits of swimmers, and remained so all the long, sweltering days." Even when they were sick, the young Muirs were held to their tasks. John contracted the mumps and could swallow no food but milk, but still he went into the fields, weak and staggering. Only when he came down with pneumonia one year was he excused from labor, though his father called no physician, saying that "God and hard work were by far the best doctors." Slave though he was, John was a willing slave; the thought of rebellion never entered his head, and he drove himself ever harder, trying to outdo the hired hands.

Still, there were moments of pleasure, moments of delight. In the spring the passenger pigeons arrived. Audubon's account of them, which John had read long ago in Scotland, still was vivid in his mind, and he watched in astonishment as great flocks of the beautiful wanderers swept thousands of acres clean of acorns in a few minutes. Long afterward he wrote of "flocks streaming south in the fall so large that they were flowing over from horizon to horizon in an almost continuous stream all day long, at the rate of forty or fifty miles an hour, like a mighty river in the sky, widening, contracting, descending like falls and cataracts, and rising suddenly here and there in huge ragged masses like high-plashing spray." The birds were wondrously good to eat, and hunters blasted them down by the thousand—but so many millions of them filled the sky that it seemed impossible to make a dent in their incredible numbers.

Then there was the boggy meadow to explore, thick with masses of flowers and busy with insects and toads. Nearby was Fountain Lake; John and his brothers built a little boat in their infrequent hours of spare time and went out sailing whenever they could get away, peering through the sunlit depths at the fishes and plants below. "On Sundays, after or before chores and sermons and Bible-lessons, we drifted about on the lake for hours," John wrote, "especially in lily time, getting finest lessons and sermons from the water and flowers, ducks, fishes, and muskrats. In particular we took Christ's advice and devoutly 'considered the lilies'—how they grow up in beauty out of gray lime mud, and ride gloriously among the breezy sun-spangles. On our way home we gathered grand bouquets of them to be kept fresh all the week."

At the south end of the lake was a shallow basin where the boys taught themselves to swim, imitating the kicking strokes of frogs. John thought he had picked up the skill, but the first time he moved out into deep water he got into trouble and sank, struggling, frightened, and confused. As soon as his feet touched bottom, 20 feet down, he kicked his way to the surface; he lost control, though, before he could get breath enough to call for help and sank again. This time water got into his lungs, and he thought he would drown; but somehow he managed, swimming underwater, to reach a part of the lake where he could stand. Humiliated by his clumsiness, he went alone back to the lake a few days later, rowed to the deepest part, "and with grim deliberation took a header and dove straight down thirty or forty feet, turned easily, and, letting my feet drag, paddled straight to the surface with my hands as father had at first directed me to do. I then swam round the boat, glorying in my suddenly acquired confidence and victory over myself, climbed into it, and dived again, with the same triumphant success. I think I went down four or five times, and each time as I made the dive-spring shouted aloud, 'Take that!' feeling that I was getting most gloriously even with myself."

There was little time for amusement, though. Except for Sundays, John had only two days a year to himself, the Fourth of July and New Year's Day, and more than half of each Sunday was taken up by church services and Bible lessons. All the other days were days of labor, rain or shine. Nor was there ever any hope of escape, it seemed. In 1856 John's elder sister Sarah married another young Scot, David Galloway, and Daniel Muir sold the Fountain Lake farm to his new son-in-law. Then Daniel bought a tract of uncleared land about four miles from the original homestead, and, John wrote, the Muirs "began all over again to clear and fence and break up other fields for a new farm, doubling all the stunting, heartbreaking chopping, grubbing, stump-digging, rail-splitting, fence-building, barn-building, house-building, and so forth." The new farm was named Hickory Hill.

John was nineteen when this second period of hard and exhausting labor began. The worst of the work descended on him and his brother David, for Daniel Muir, growing old, had decided to devote most of his time to Bible study, preaching, and prayer meetings. John was strong and tireless, priding himself on his ability to endure all that was put upon him, but nevertheless he was showing signs of inward rebellion against his father's stern demands. The contradictions between what Daniel preached and what he practiced particularly incensed John, for his father advocated a religion of love and simplicity, yet in his love for wealth and landowning he ruthlessly drove farm animals to death and turned his children virtually into slaves. Daniel had even sold Jack, his sons' pony, when a man heading for the California gold mines offered a good price for him. Nor were Daniel's equally God-fearing neighbors any better; they, too, gave loud praise to the Lord but treated their families and their livestock with callous indifference. The bigotry and coldness of these pious Scots left John with a distaste for any sort of formal, organized religion; though he had strong religious feelings himself, he preferred to express them privately, far from churches, ministers, and dogma.

His mind was opening in these years to the world of knowledge, to that world beyond the Bible that his father rejected. The summer he was fifteen John took up higher arithmetic, buying a textbook and giving himself lessons from it each day for a few minutes after lunch. Quickly he mastered it and went on to algebra, geometry, and trigonometry. In 1854, when he was sixteen, two boys from nearby farms awakened John to the beauties of poetry, chanting their favorite verses to him while he and they were building a log road across a swamp. Hearing the magical words, he made "a great and sudden discovery that the poetry of the Bible, Shakespeare, and Milton was a source of inspiring, exhilarating, uplifting pleasure, and I became anxious to know all the poets, and saved up small sums to buy as many of their books as possible."

Books were hard to come by in that pioneer community, but John did manage to purchase a few volumes of poetry, which he read whenever he could steal five or ten minutes from his chores. William Duncan, a kindly farmer who lived two miles away, learned of John's new love of books and let him borrow a good many, chiefly the *Waverley* novels of Sir Walter Scott. These had to be hidden from Daniel, who believed that fiction was "the spawn of Satan, the Devil's own book of lies."

Daniel could be persuaded to buy books for John, so long as they were serious and Godly works. Thus he was talked into obtaining Josephus' *The Jewish*

War and D'Aubigné's *History of the Reformation,* but he balked when John asked for Plutarch's *Lives,* saying that he wanted no part of "the old pagan." Fortunately, Daniel just then had become deeply interested in a food fad, giving up meat in favor of a vegetarian diet. John suggested to his father "that Plutarch might be turned to account on the food question by revealing what those old Greeks and Romans ate to make them strong." Daniel took the bait, "and so at last we gained our glorious Plutarch," Muir wrote. Plutarch held no clues to the diet of the ancients, and meat was banned from the Muir household until John made use of his own extensive Biblical learning to shake his father's vegetarianism: He pointed out to Daniel that when the prophet Elijah had gone into hiding, God had sent ravens to bring him bread and meat. If God had supplied one of His own prophets with meat, it must surely be acceptable food for ordinary mortals. Daniel bowed to the authority of the Scriptures.

Through one ruse and another John succeeded in acquiring a well-rounded library despite his father's oft-proclaimed belief that "the Bible is the only book human beings can possibly require throughout all the journey from earth to heaven." But finding time to read them was a different problem. The family rule was that everyone was to go to sleep after evening prayers, and in winter bedtime came as early as eight o'clock. John used to linger in the kitchen with a book and candle after the others had retired, but usually he got no more than five minutes' reading done before his father noticed the light and ordered him off to bed. "Father failed perhaps two or three times in a whole winter to notice my light for nearly ten minutes, magnificent golden blocks of time, long to be remembered like holidays or geological history," Muir wrote. Finally Daniel wearied of this nightly struggle with his son's love of reading. Although he remained inflexible about the hour of bedtime, he gave John the privilege of getting up as early as he wished to read.

The night that privilege was granted, John went to bed at eight, hoping "that somebody or something might call me out of sleep to avail myself of this wonderful indulgence." Though usually he slept until his father summoned him, this night he was surprised to find himself awakening of his own accord, and, rushing downstairs to check the kitchen clock, he discovered to his delight that it was only one in the morning! "Five hours to myself!" he cried. "Five huge, solid hours!" Night after night the same thing happened: Some mysterious alarm clock within his soul awakened him at one, and from then till dawn his time was his own. Though he had abruptly cut his hours of sleep from ten to only five a night, he felt no ill effects. His father heard him moving about the house in the small hours but said nothing for two weeks. Finally, though, he insisted on knowing what time John was getting up. About one, John said, in a meek, guilty voice. What kind of time was that, Daniel demanded, for awakening? John merely reminded him of the permission he had granted for him to get up whenever he pleased. "I *know* it," Daniel said, "I *know* I gave you that miserable permission, but I never imagined that you would get up in the middle of the night."

John continued to awaken early, not only to read but also to spend time in his cellar workshop, for he had developed remarkable mechanical skills in his middle teens. He had started with a few tools his father had brought from Scotland—a vise, some files, a hammer, a coarse-toothed saw, chisels, and such. He made awls, punches, and a pair of compasses from pieces of wire and broken files and fashioned a fine-toothed saw out of a strip of steel from an old corset. With this equipment he set out to be an inventor. Having spent so many years in backbreaking manual labor, he had a special interest in creating automatic devices: His first invention was a miniature self-setting sawmill, which he tested satisfactorily by damming a little stream in a meadow. "This invention," he wrote, "was speedily followed by a lot of others—water-wheels, curious doorlocks and latches, thermometers, hygrometers, pyrometers, clocks, a barometer, an automatic contrivance for feeding the horses at any required hour, a lamp-lighter and fire-lighter, an early-or-late rising machine, and so forth."

He devoted much of his time in 1856 to his "early-or-late rising machine." This astonishing clockwork mechanism was designed to tell time and strike like an ordinary clock; to register the day of the week and the day of the month; to light fires and lamps at preset times through an arrangement of cogs and levers; and, most amazingly, to serve as an alarm clock by upending a bed at the hour the sleeper wished to arise! Though he had never seen the inside of any sort of clock or watch, John planned his machine by studying the laws of pendulums in a book and proceeded to carve all the necessary parts out of wood. He kept the machine hidden in a spare upstairs bedroom while working on it, but one day his father discovered it and asked to know what it was. John explained. "Do you not think it is very wrong to waste your time on such nonsense?" Daniel demanded.

"No," John said, "I don't think I'm doing any wrong."

"Well," his father replied, "I assure you I do; and if you were only half as zealous in the study of religion as you are in contriving and whittling these useless, nonsensical things, it would be infinitely better for you."

John thought his father would burn the machine, but Daniel did not have the heart to destroy it, and soon John succeeded in finishing it. One day at noon he set it up in the parlor, hung two rocks on it as weights, and started it running. Then he went out to haul grain to the barn. John learned from one of his sisters that as soon as the clock struck, Daniel emerged from his study, got down on his knees before his son's device, and carefully examined its workings, clearly proud of John's ability to invent and build such a thing.

Having made one, he quickly made another along the same lines, far more elegant in appearance and inscribed with a Biblical phrase intended to please his father. The whole family admired it, and more than fifty years later it was still functioning perfectly in John Muir's California home.

Next came a large clock with four dials and hands 14 feet long; John intended to mount it on the peak of the barn roof so that it could be read from the fields, but Daniel would not let him put it up, claiming that it would attract too many curiosity seekers. To his great disappointment he had to abandon the project. But even Daniel was compelled to appreciate the thermometer John built out of a thick rod of iron 3 feet long. Changes in temperature caused the rod to expand or contract, and a system of levers registered these changes, multiplied some 32,000 times, on a broad dial. The thermometer was so sensitive that when anyone approached with 4 or 5 feet of it, the heat of the observer's body made the pointer of the dial vibrate. The clever combination locks that John devised for the barn were less of a success in the family. One day he rode off to town with a load of grain, leaving the doors locked; a sudden rainstorm came up while his brothers were in the fields, and they rushed for the barn, but they had no idea how to operate the locks and received a drenching.

As his skills developed and his mind matured, a great restlessness took possession of John Muir. He had no wish to leave his gentle mother, his brothers, and his much-beloved elder sister Margaret, but he knew that he could not spend his life as Daniel Muir's farmhand. His mother hoped he would enter the ministry; Margaret believed he was destined to be a great inventor; John himself had no clear idea of what he wanted to do, though sometimes he fancied he would become a physician. For that, though, he needed a university education, and without money he could not have that. Perhaps, he thought, he could bring in enough income from his inventions to pay for his tuition. But he did not know how to go about that, and so in 1859 he celebrated his twenty-first birthday at Hickory Hill with his future uncertain.

In the summer of 1860 his book-lending friend, the farmer William Duncan, offered a suggestion. That September the Wisconsin State Agricultural Fair would open in the city of Madison. Why not exhibit some of his inventions there? He was bound to attract great attention with them, and surely the proprietor of some machine shop would offer him a job. John agreed. He would go out into the world, taking his machines with him, and seek his fortune. When he told Daniel of his decision, he asked if he could count on his father for financial help if he fell into need—but, predictably, Daniel refused, saying, "Depend entirely on yourself." Many years later, John Muir commented that this was "good advice, I suppose, but surely needlessly severe for a bashful, home-loving boy who had worked so hard." As he set forth, then, John's cash assets amounted to about $10 that he had saved over the years, and a British gold sovereign, worth $5, that his grandfather had given him upon his departure for America eleven years before.

In the fall of 1860, while a tall, awkward-looking man named Abraham Lincoln was opening his campaign to become President of the United States, John Muir bade farewell to his family—his father icily refused to see him off—and loaded his heavy pack of inventions into a wagon. He was a sturdy, powerful figure, somewhat eccentric-looking in his rough country clothes, with a tangle of hair dangling down to his shoulders and a wild, untrimmed beard. His brother David drove him to the railroad station at the town of Pardeeville—which, though it was only nine miles from home, John had never seen before. He stayed there overnight, and the next day, with a clatter of pistons and a sulfurous blast of smoke, the train for Madison came roaring down the track. He surrendered his bulky bundle of machinery to the baggagemaster, and then, the better to profit by the ride, he wangled permission to travel in the locomotive, next to the engineer and all his fascinating controls. And off he went to win his place in the world.

3

On His Own

In Madison, Muir made his way to the 40-acre fairgrounds on foot, with his pack slung over his shoulder, and arranged to place his mechanical wonders on display in the building known as the Temple of Art. He set up his clocks and his thermometer in the final moments before the fair's official opening. Then the blare of military bands was heard, and thousands of people—more people than John Muir had ever seen in one place in his life—came flooding through the gates.

Many of them paused in amazement in front of Muir's exhibit. Two small boys, the sons of professors at the nearby University of Wisconsin, had volunteered to help him demonstrate his early-rising machine. They lay down in a bed that Muir had attached to the device, while he set the clock a few minutes ahead and explained to the crowd in his thick Scots brogue what was about to happen. When the proper time came, the wheels and levers went into action, elevating the head of the bed to an angle of 45 degrees and catapulting the boys out upon their feet. This always drew laughter and applause from the throng. The sensitivity of Muir's big thermometer also gained much praise.

Local newspapers gave him enthusiastic coverage. One headed its article "An Ingenious Whittler," and another declared that Muir's inventions were "surprising, and could only have been executed by genuine genius." When these pieces appeared, the crowds around his display grew even larger. On the third day, a newspaper noted, the area was "so thronged that a passage could only be gained by strong pushing." His were by far the most popular exhibits, and when the fair closed, he was awarded a prize of $15. The chairman of the judging committee commented, "The clocks presented by J. Muir exhibited great ingenuity. The Committee regard him as a genius in the best sense, and think the state should feel a pride in encouraging him."

As he had hoped, the attention he attracted at the fair brought him several offers of jobs. The one that seemed most attractive came from a certain Norman Wiard, who had invented a flat-bottomed boat designed to run by steam power on the ice-covered surfaces of the frozen rivers of the northern states. Wiard, who had exhibited his iceboat at the fair, was about to test it for the first time on the Mississippi near the town of Prairie du Chien, Wisconsin, and he hired Muir as his assistant. After the fair, Muir sent word to his family of his new employment and went with Wiard to Prairie du Chien to wait for the river to freeze.

While living in Prairie du Chien, he supported himself with odd jobs—looking after someone's cow and horse and doing chores at the Mondell House, the hotel where he was lodging. When his mother learned that he was staying at such a fashionable place, she decided he needed a suit of store-bought clothes so that he would not look too rustic, and Daniel Muir, surprisingly, agreed, purchasing a costly outfit and shipping it to his son. But the Mondell House was a trifle too fashionable for John Muir. The young people of the town went there in the evening to dance to the music of a pianist and even played kissing games—which shocked someone brought up as strictly as he had been. One night, unable to stand the sinful merriment any longer, he denounced the pleasure seekers for their "worldliness and silly talk," condemning them with lengthy Biblical quotations. But they stared at the earnest, solemn farm boy in astonishment and went on with their amusements.

The doings of Mr. Wiard left Muir equally uncomfortable. He had hoped to learn a great deal in Wiard's machine shop, but the shop was rarely open, and when the celebrated iceboat finally underwent its maiden voyage, it broke down almost at once. Repairs were made, but still the boat went nowhere. Soon the Prairie du Chien newspapers were speaking of the inventor as "the notorious Mr. Wiard" and calling his boat "a humbug." Late in January, 1861, Muir admitted to himself that the project was hopeless and boarded a train for Madison. It was still his ambition to enter the university there. As he watched the students coming and going with their books, he wrote, "I thought that if I could only join them it would be the greatest joy of life. I was desperately hungry and thirsty for knowledge and willing to endure anything to get it."

In Madison he earned a few dollars by making and selling some early-rising machines and worked at occasional menial jobs. He was too shy, though, to go near the university, until a student who had noticed his machines at the fair spoke to him and told him that very little money, really, was needed to enroll. And so, "with fear and trembling, overladen with ignorance," Muir went to see the dean and apply for admission. He explained that he had had no formal schooling since the age of eleven, when he had left Scotland, but the dean did not see that as an obstacle: The university had a special preparatory department for students who had not completed their high school courses, and Muir could be entered in that immediately. He had educated himself so well, however, that within a few weeks he was transferred to the regular freshman class. He signed up for chemistry and geology classes taught by Dr. Ezra Slocum Carr and for courses in Latin and Greek given by Dr. James Davie Butler. They happened to be the fathers of the small boys who had helped him demonstrate his invention at the fair; he had met both professors at that time and had been invited more than once to their homes as a guest.

He moved into a second-floor room in North Hall, the men's dormitory, and promptly became a campus celebrity. Older than most of the other students but far less sophisticated, a backwoods bumpkin with long, unruly hair and a Scots accent, he seemed strange and wild to them. "If I had a beard like yours," one of his classmates told him, "I would set fire to it!" But he came to the university with the reputation as a genius that he had gained at the state fair, and enhanced it by filling his room with strange machines. One of these was an improved version of his early-rising device, operated not by clockwork but by sunbeams. This he accomplished, he wrote, "by taking a lens out of my small spy-glass, fixing it on a frame on the sill of my bedroom window, and pointing it to the sunrise; the sunbeams focused on a thread burned it through, allowing the bed machinery to put me on my feet. When I wished to arise at any given time after sunrise, I had only to turn the pivoted frame that held the lens the requisite number of degrees or minutes."

Another of Muir's gadgets was his mischievous "loafer's chair"—equipped with a concealed spring that fired a gun loaded with blank cartridges whenever some unsuspecting victim sat down and leaned back too far. But his masterpiece was an automatic study desk, nine feet high. This elaborate construction, composed of a large central wheel and a multitude of cogs and pegs, was triggered each morning by one of his many clocks. The central wheel turned, and the first book to be studied was pushed up from a rack below by a mechanical hand and thrown open at the proper place. It was permitted to remain there for fifteen minutes. Then, Muir tells us, "the machinery closed the book and allowed it to drop back into its stall, then moved the rack forward and threw up the next in order, and so on, all the day being divided according to the times of recitation, and time required and allotted to each study." One of Muir's college roommates of later years wrote that it was amusing to see him sitting there "as if chained, working like a beaver against the clock and desk."

Muir's poverty complicated his existence. A year's tuition cost $32—a huge sum in 1861, when a wage of just a few dollars a week was considered adequate. Beyond this, he needed to buy books and to pay for the acids, flasks, glass tubing, and other equipment his chemistry course required. His slender savings soon were exhausted, even though he cut his food expenditures to 50 cents a week and dined mainly on graham crackers and water. In March he was forced to write to his father for money. Though Daniel Muir was willing enough to contribute liberally to organizations bringing the Bible to far-off heathen lands, he offered his son, at first, nothing more than pious advice: "Practice economy in all that you do. . . . See that all you do is founded upon Scripture." John by now was taking what he later called "a course in starvation." Writing to his sister Sarah, he said, "A body has an extraordinary amount of longfaced sober scheming and thought to get butter and bread." His skimpy diet undermined his health, and when word of this finally reached his family,

Daniel sent him $10, saying, "Let me know when you are in great distress and I will try what I can do." Later in the spring he sent $50 more, and another $40 in June. Behind his stern mask, John admitted, his father was "foundationally kind."

In April, 1861, midway through Muir's first semester of college, came the attack by Southern forces on the government base at Fort Sumter, South Carolina, that touched off the Civil War. President Lincoln called for 75,000 volunteers for the army, and on the war's first day eight University of Wisconsin upperclassmen enlisted. The fairgrounds next to the university became Camp Randall, a military training installation where, shortly, platoons of soldiers were drilling and marching. Muir remained aloof from the excitement. His strong religious feelings and powerful pacifist convictions made warfare impossible for him; regardless of the moral issues involved in the war, he knew he could never bring himself to kill another human being for the sake of patriotism. So he ignored the hubbub of Camp Randall and stuck diligently to his studies.

When classes ended for the summer, he went back to the Hickory Hill farm. His family scarcely recognized him, for he had been gone nearly a year and showed up now wearing his unfamiliar city clothes. Daniel had agreed to pay him 75 cents a day for a summer's labor in the fields, but for this noble wage John had to work with heroic energy, harvesting four acres of wheat every day. His stories of college life so impressed his brother David that when he returned to the university in the autumn, David accompanied him to enroll as a freshman.

The pressures of the war were increasingly transforming every aspect of civilian life. Muir now often visited Camp Randall to talk to the young recruits and offer them religious counseling. He was troubled by their enthusiasm for battle, and complained to a friend that the soldiers were going to war "on a half-dance, with a smile on their faces, and . . . a loud laugh." He urged them to take deeper thought of what they were about to do. "If the whole abominable business is necessary," he wrote, "if we must cut the throats of the Secessionists, let it be done solemnly. . . ."

Financial problems forced John and David to drop out of the university temporarily during the winter of 1861-62. They both took jobs as country schoolmasters—David finding a position near Madison and John being hired by a community 10 miles away—and continued their university work by studying on their own at night. John's salary was $20 a month plus room and board. The subject he taught was science; he performed chemical experiments for his classes and delighted them with his clocks and other inventions. Among his new gadgets was a clock made out of a tin pail and a coin: "It cost about two hours work," he wrote, "and kept time by water passing in a fine jet through a three-cent piece." He also devised a wheel-shaped instrument that hung above the blackboard and dropped a shingle to signal the end of each class period, and a complicated contraption that lit a fire in the schoolhouse stove every morning by tipping a vial of sulfuric acid onto a teaspoonful of sugar mixed with potassium chlorate. His lectures were popular with his students, and he won such fame that soon he was being invited to speak in neighboring school districts. "He had chestnut-brown hair hanging to his shoulders," wrote one of his pupils, "and a long unkempt beard, and a rough ungroomed look even for that day when most folks didn't dress very well." But his grasp of science was firm, and his explanations were clear and interesting.

In March, 1862, he was able to go back to the university, although David, finding college work too much for him, did not. It was a somber time. No longer was Camp Randall full of laughing, dashing recruits in elegant new uniforms, impatient to be off to war. Now sick and wounded soldiers were being shipped back from the battlefront, and the camp was a place for the crippled and maimed and for victims of smallpox, typhoid, and pneumonia. Soldiers were dying there at a rate of one a day. The sound of funeral drums and the crack of ceremonial muskets were heard constantly in Madison. When 139 ailing Confederate prisoners arrived in May, putting a dangerous strain on the overloaded hospital facilities, the death rate climbed tenfold. The daily tragedies of Camp Randall left a deep mark on John Muir. Witnessing such needless destruction of life, he vowed to do what he could to become a saver of lives and pledged himself definitely to the study of medicine. His friend and adviser Dr. Ezra Slocum Carr recommended that he study chemistry for another year in Madison to prepare himself for entering the University of Michigan Medical School at Ann Arbor. For the first time, he had a clear goal.

Because the University of Wisconsin did not then have adequate equipment for the sort of advanced chemical research Muir wanted to do, he turned his dormitory room into a private chemistry lab, spending whatever he earned on the apparatus he needed. But also, though he knew it would be of no use to him as a physician, he developed an intense interest in geology. This was something instilled in him by Dr. Carr, who took him on field trips to nearby lakes and hills and showed him how the forces of nature had helped shape the landscape. Dr. Carr had an extensive library of books on geology which he lent to Muir; among them were works by the Swiss scientist Louis Agassiz, setting forth the theory of glaciation, which Muir found particularly exciting. Agassiz believed that in prehistoric times the earth had experienced prolonged periods of extremely cold weather, during which glaciers—rivers of ice—had covered much of Europe and North America. A "universal ice sheet," Agassiz claimed, had flowed down from the North Pole, burying the land to a depth of a mile or more. He had searched for evidence of this ice sheet throughout the 1830's and 1840's and claimed to have found it in the form of scratches and grooves on rocks and deposits of boulders and rubble scattered across the countryside. The glacial theory was a controversial one because it seemed to contradict the Bible, in which no mention of a great ice age could be detected. Despite his own intense education in Biblical teachings—or perhaps because of it—Muir was immediately captivated by the image of a world engulfed in glaciers. Though aware that his father would be aghast at the idea that he was studying such blasphemous stuff, he read everything available on the subject.

Muir was also extending his knowledge of literature and philosophy. His guide in this was Professor Carr's wife, Mrs. Jeanne Carr—an attractive, intelligent woman about ten years older than himself. She welcomed him to the Carr home and gave him free access to their well-stocked bookshelves—directing him particularly to poets such as Wordsworth and philosophers like Thoreau and Ralph Waldo Emerson, whose concern it was to interpret the relationship between nature and man. Through their books Muir developed a sense of the harmony and unity of all things, the divine balance that was to be found in nature—and which man so often destroyed.

To these interests suddenly was added a passion for botany that threatened to push everything else aside. Muir had always responded to the beauty of trees and flowers but had never studied them in any systematic way. One day in June, 1862, though, he was standing with his classmate Milton Griswold outside their dormitory when Griswold, whose hobby was botany, reached up and plucked a flower from a branch of a locust tree. He asked Muir if he knew what family the tree belonged to, and when Muir admitted ignorance of such matters, Griswold launched into a discussion of the locust tree's close relationship to such humble plants as the pea vine and the vetch. He showed how the arrangement of flowers and leaves was similar in all members of the pea family, to which the locust belonged, pointing out that there was nothing arbitrary about the classification of plants into families. "Nature has attended to all that," Griswold said, "giving essential unity with boundless variety, so that the botanist has only to examine plants to learn the harmony of their relations."

This notion coincided so well with the ideas Muir had gained from Mrs. Carr's books of philosophy that he found himself hungry to know more about the world of plants. Griswold's brief botany lesson, he wrote, "charmed me and sent me flying to the woods and meadows in wild enthusiasm. . . . I wandered away at every opportunity, making long excursions round the lakes, gathering specimens and keeping them fresh in a bucket in my room to study at night after my regular class tasks were learned; for my eyes never closed on the plant glory I had seen." He bought a botany text and spent much of his time collecting, sorting, and classifying wild flowers, finding in them "glorious traces of the thoughts of God" that led him "on and on into the infinite cosmos."

His dormitory room began to look like a branch of the college museum. Charles Vroman, who was his roommate in the spring of 1862, wrote that the room "was lined with shelves, one above the other, higher than a man could reach. These shelves were filled with retorts, glass tubes, glass jars, botanical and geological specimens, and small mechanical contrivances. On the floor around the sides of the room were a number of machines of larger size whose purposes were not apparent at a glance, but which I came to know later." Vroman described Muir as "gentle and loving," and "the most cheerful, happy-hearted man I ever knew." Another classmate of this time spoke of him as "a storage battery of energy, encased in flexible, elastic steel."

But wartime tensions and his own self-imposed schedule of rigorous overwork were taking their toll on him. He was depressed by the unending slaughter on the battlefields, and now he feared that he would be drafted and forced to take part in that slaughter himself. He spent the summer of 1862 on the old family farm at Fountain Lake, working for his brother-in-law David Galloway and going forth every morning at dawn to collect plant specimens, but even during this relatively tranquil time a mood of despair was rising in him. When he returned to the University of Wisconsin that fall, he discovered a new source of anxiety: The school was in a crisis over money and might have to close its doors, in which case, he wrote to the Galloways, "I should have to leave Madison for some institution which has not yet been wounded to death by our war-demon." The university remained open, but all through the final months of 1862 and the first ones of 1863 his feelings of mental stress and fatigue mounted. In the fall of 1863 he was supposed to enter medical school, yet the strain of that new challenge now appeared too much for him. The only remedy he saw was to get away from his studies, into the nourishing wilderness. So he began to plan to spend that summer in a "geological and botanical ramble" down the Wisconsin River to the Mississippi and on southward. "I am not so well as I was last term," he told the Galloways. "I need a rest. Perhaps my tour will do me good, though a three or four hundred mile walk with a load is not, at least in appearance, much of a rest."

He set out in June, 1863, the day after classes ended. Originally he intended to hike alone, but two of his classmates named Rice and Blake asked to accompany him. The trio followed the steep gorge of the Wisconsin, scrambling daringly across high bluffs and boulder-strewn slopes so that Muir could have a close look at what he called the "rock scriptures." He climbed, a friend said, "like a human spider," but Rice, less agile, sprained his ankle badly and had to be sent home by train. Muir and Blake went on into Iowa and south along the Mississippi, loading their packs with plants and fossils. The great river was full of huge logs, chained together and floating downstream toward sawmills; looking at these fallen forest giants, Muir felt a touch of horror and wondered if a time would come when there would be no trees left to cut.

Weary at last of trekking on foot, he and Blake decided to buy a small boat and paddle their way homeward. They got up the Mississippi without much difficulty, but they were unable to defeat the powerful current at the place where the Wisconsin River empties into the Father of Waters; they abandoned their boat and hiked to the nearest town, where Blake bought a stagecoach ticket back to Madison. Muir continued to walk, going by way of Prairie du Chien. There he hoped to visit a girl he had known in 1861, niece of the owner of the fashionable hotel, the Mondell House; but her uncle evidently felt it was best not to let the strange young man meet her again, and Muir moved on, rebuffed and discouraged. Late in July he went to Madison to remove his belongings from the university dormitory. The Carrs were out of town, but he paid a call on his other faculty friend, Dr. Butler, the professor of Latin and Greek. As a farewell gift to a favorite pupil, Dr. Butler offered Muir his own copy of the nature poems of Virgil to take on future wanderings, but Muir refused the book, explaining that he wished to view nature through his own eyes, not Virgil's.

By early August he was with Sarah and David Galloway at the Fountain Lake farm. He intended to work for his brother-in-law for the rest of the summer and present himself in the fall at the University of Michigan Medical School, which had accepted him although he had received no degree at Wisconsin. But autumn came, and Muir stayed on at Fountain Lake. He could not bring himself to return to the classroom. A strange paralysis of the will gripped him. One problem was the draft: President Lincoln was calling for more and more soldiers, and Muir expected to be taken momentarily. The prospect of becoming a soldier plunged him into such gloom that he was unable to do anything. He was even more deeply troubled, though, by the entire question of what he proposed to do with his life. He was twenty-five years old. He had done a little studying, a little inventing, a little roaming, but he had mastered no profession, had formed few lasting friendships, had taken no steps toward marriage. "I was tormented with soul hunger," he wrote a few years later. "I began to doubt whether I was fully born. . . . I was on the world. But was I in it?" He was assailed by "vague unrest and longings." To practice medicine, he saw, would be a fine way of serving his fellowman, but it would also be an imprisonment. He did not want to surrender his freedom to wander.

What he really wanted to do, he realized, was to tramp the wilderness, "not as a mere sport or plaything excursion, but to find the Law that governs the relations subsisting between human beings and Nature." The endless round of daily work was not for him. "Civilization," he said, "has not much to brag about. It drives its victims in flocks, repressing the growth of individuality."

So he let medical school go by. In February, 1864,

still at Fountain Lake, he wrote to a friend, "With study and labor I have scarcely been at all sensible of the flight of time since I reached home. In my walks to and from my field work and in occasional rambles I, of course, searched every inch of ground for botanical specimens which, preserved in water, were analyzed at night. My task was seldom completed before twelve or one o'clock." A few weeks later, as spring neared, he felt it was time to begin a new ramble. To the same friend he wrote that he still planned to take up medicine eventually, saying that he had "by no means given up all hope of still finding an opportunity to pursue this favorite study some other time." But that time would never come. In a letter of March 1, 1864, he wrote, "I am to take the cars in about half an hour. I really do not know where I shall halt. I feel like Milton's Adam and Eve—'The world was all before them where to choose their place of rest.' "

4

Beginning to Roam

"I quietly wandered away," Muir wrote, "happy and free, poor and rich." The journal of his 1864 travels has not survived, and some careful detective work was needed to reconstruct his route. Almost seventy years later his friend and biographer William Badé located a collection of botanical specimens that Muir had gathered on this trip and had left behind, forgotten, in an Indianapolis attic in 1867. Each specimen was neatly tagged with the date and place where Muir had collected it, and from this Badé was able to tell where Muir had gone.

Canada had been his first destination. Walking with a long loping stride, maintaining a steady but unhurried pace, he went northward across Wisconsin and eastward along the upper reaches of Lake Michigan and Lake Huron into Ontario. Then, moving southward through the chain of islands between Lake Huron and Georgian Bay, he headed toward the Lake Simcoe region. The entire area was full of lakes and swamps carved by the retreating glaciers of the last ice age, and Muir found fascination everywhere. One scrap of memorandum that survives from this period notes his pleasure at the seven and a half hours he spent in the "solitudes extraordinary" of a cedar swamp dotted with beaver meadows: "I shall not soon forget the chaos of fallen trees in all stages of decay and the tangled branches of the white cedars through which I had to force my way; nor the feeling with which I observed the sun wheeling to the west while yet above, beneath, and around all was silence and the seemingly endless harvest of the swamp."

For food he made do with bread, with oatmeal flakes, or with tea leaves, which he chewed and washed down with cold water. The farmers he met, most of them Irish or Scottish, usually were hospitable, though they had difficulty understanding why he was tramping through their country. "Botany" was an unknown word to them. "If told that I was collecting plants, they would desire to know whether it was cabbage plants that I sought, and if so, how could I find cabbage plants in the bush?" he wrote, "Others took me for a government official of some kind, or minister, or peddler." In one town, "far in the dark maple woods," he was surprised to discover some emigrants from his native town of Dunbar and spent a pleasant day with them catching up on gossip from Scotland.

In June he stopped at the farm of a family called Campbell, hoping to buy a day's bread, but the Campbells, seeing how gaunt and mud-stained he was, insisted that he stay awhile with them. He was their guest for a month, easing his conscience by helping with the field chores. Using their home as a base, he prowled almost inaccessible swamps, struggling through tangled branches and over heaps of dead trees. On one of these excursions he found himself so deep in the bog in late afternoon that he feared he would not reach dry ground by nightfall and started to look around for a tree in which he could perch, monkeylike, until morning. Trudging on, weary and discouraged, he suddenly came upon a rare orchid, *Calypso borealis,* "the hider of the North," growing from a bed of yellow mosses on the bank of a stream. He had long hoped for a glimpse of this elusive bloom, and there it was. Many years later, writing of this incident, he said, "The flower was white and made the impression of the utmost simple purity like a snowflower. No other bloom was near it, for the bog a short distance below the surface was still frozen, and the water was ice cold. It seemed the most spiritual of all the flower people I had ever met. I sat down beside it and fairly cried for joy. . . . Hunger and weariness vanished, and only after the sun was low in the west I plashed on through the swamp, strong and exhilarated as if never more to feel any mortal care." Stumbling out of the swamp at last as night fell, he came to a farmer's log cabin and was warmly received. The farmer's wife was astonished to learn that he had gone into the swamp, where so many travelers had become lost and perished, merely to search for flowers. "She wondered how plants could draw me to these awful places," he wrote, "and said, 'It's God's mercy ye ever got out.' "

In late July he left the Campbells and started south toward Niagara Falls. Each night he camped in the forest; only once was the deep peace of the wilderness broken, one cold night about midnight when his campfire burned low and a pack of wolves came sniffing close. Muir threw a log at one large gray wolf less than 10 feet away from him, and the animals retreated; then he sat up, listening warily to their howling conversations, until daybreak.

The beginning of September saw him on the heights overlooking Niagara Falls. There he was joined by his brother Dan, who had spent the summer working in a Canadian sawmill. He bore news from home: The draft calls had been increased again, and their mother did not want either of them to return to the United States so long as they were in danger of being taken into military service. With winter coming on, Muir needed a place to stay, and, since he had exhausted his funds, he chose to seek employment at the sawmill where Dan had worked.

The mill was at Trout Hollow, a dell on Lake Huron's Georgian Bay near the town of Meaford, Canada. William Trout, a Scot four years older than John Muir, was its owner. He was about to enlarge a rake factory connected with the mill, and he gladly hired both brothers, taking John on as a mechanic at a wage of $10 a month plus room and board.

They moved into the Trout house. Muir mounted

his bed on an axle and rigged it, as usual, to an alarm clock that was set to put him on his feet at five every morning; if he happened to be sleeping diagonally when the bed upended itself, he sometimes was thrown to the floor. "The fall of John's bed," Trout wrote, "was a wake-up signal for everyone in the house. If we heard a double shock, caused by a roll-out, we had the signal for a good laugh on John." He divided his time between work and botanizing, going on long expeditions in the dense forests along the bay until winter interfered. In the spring he resumed his explorations, glorying in the wealth of birds and wild flowers. The Trouts were members of the Disciples of Christ and asked him to teach a Sunday school class; he agreed, on the condition that he be allowed to teach science rather than religion, and took troops of delighted boys with him on exciting field trips in the woods.

In May, 1865, when the expansion of the rake factory was finished, Dan Muir left Trout Hollow. He was eager to go to college and needed to earn more money than Trout could pay. But John remained, though he was "touched with melancholy and loneliness" by his brother's departure. He was still the prisoner of his soul's uncertainties. Medical school now seemed an impossibility to him, but he did have some hope of returning to complete his studies at the University of Wisconsin, provided it would take him in without charging tuition. Evidently the university was willing to admit him on this basis, but the letter notifying him of the dean's favorable decision never reached him, though he "waited and wearied for it a long time" in the winter of 1864-65. Nothing else seemed open to him except a renewed period of forest wandering, but even for that he would need more money than he had been able to save. Therefore, in the summer of 1865, he signed a contract with Trout binding him to produce 30,000 broom handles and 12,000 rakes, using highly efficient machinery of his own design. For this he would receive half the profits from the sale of the goods.

A letter he wrote that September to his good friend of university days Mrs. Jeanne Carr indicates his restlessness and uneasiness. "I seem to be able to do but one thing at a time," he complained. "Since undertaking, a month or two ago, to invent new machinery for our mill, my mind seems so to bury itself in the work that I am fit for but little else; and then a lifetime is so little a time that we die ere we get ready to live."

He was twenty-seven now, and felt the months devouring his "handful of hasty years." But what could he do? "I would like to go to college," he told Mrs. Carr, "but then I have to say to myself, 'You will die ere you can do anything else.' I should like to invent useful machinery, but it comes, 'You do not wish to spend your lifetime among machines and you will die ere you can do anything else.' I should like to study medicine that I might do my part in lessening human misery, but again it comes, 'You will die ere you are ready to be able to do so.' "

For all his despair, he astounded Trout with his mechanical skills. He built, first, a self-feeding lathe that could turn out eight handles a minute, 2,500 a day, doubling the factory's previous output. Then he fashioned automatic devices to make rake teeth and set them in place. In November he wrote that he was "busy almost to craziness . . . inventing machinery twenty-four hours a day." The 30,000 broom handles were done by February, 1866, and were stored in the factory for final seasoning while he worked on the rakes. In a few weeks 6,000 rakes were assembled; he had only 6,000 more to do, and he would be free again to roam.

But on the night of March 1, a spark from a cabin chimney landed on the factory roof, and shortly the entire place was ablaze. There was no way to save the building: Factory, machinery, rakes, brooms, Muir's notebooks—everything was lost, and nothing had been insured. Trout invited Muir to help rebuild the plant and share as a partner in his profits, but he could not abide remaining there any longer. Sadly he said that he would have to move on, though he had only enough money to pay his fare back to the United States. Trout promised to give him $200 for his services and eventually made good on that promise; but it was a sorry ending to months of hard work.

Muir chose now to go to Indianapolis, picking it almost at random because it was an important manufacturing center and was likely to have employment for a man who knew something about machinery. He arrived in May, 1866, and found a job at once with Osgood, Smith & Co., a company that produced hubs, spokes, and other parts for carriage wheels. It took him on at $10 a week; but within a few days his skill and speed became apparent, and he was placed in charge of the big circular saws at a salary of $18 a week. Not long afterward, when he showed that he was capable of redesigning and improving the factory's lathes and saws, he was promoted again, and his pay was raised to the unusually high figure, for that era, of $25 a week.

"I never before felt so *utterly homeless* as now," he wrote his sister Sarah Galloway during his first weeks in Indianapolis. "I do not feel sad, but I cannot find a good boarding-place, to say nothing of a home, and so I have not yet unpacked my trunk, and am at any moment as ready to leave this house for a march as were the Israelites while eating the passover. Much as I love the peace and quiet of retirement, I *feel* something within, some restless fires that urge me on in a way very different from my *real* wishes, and I suppose that I am doomed to live in some of these noisy commercial centers. . . . Now that I am among machines I begin to feel that I have some talent that way, and so I almost think, unless things change soon, I shall turn my whole mind into that channel." But in the same letter he told of gathering wild flowers a mile and a half outside town before breakfast that day: "When I first entered the woods and stood among the beautiful flowers and trees of God's own garden, so pure and chaste and lovely, I could not help shedding tears of joy." Machines would not be able to hold him for long.

His loneliness soon was lessened. Dr. Butler of the University of Wisconsin had given him a letter of introduction to the Merrills, a wealthy and influential Indianapolis family, which said of him, among other things, "If you walk the fields with him, you will find that Solomon could not speak more wisely about plants." It took Muir some time to overcome his shyness, but later in the spring of 1866 he presented himself at the Merrill house and received a warm welcome. Before long he was leading the young Merrills and their cousins and friends on nature trips in the woods outside town.

At the factory he was rapidly rising to an executive position. He invented a machine that automatically assembled hubs and spokes into complete carriage wheels but declined to patent it, saying, "I believe all improvements and inventions should be the property of the human race. No inventor has the right to profit by an invention for which he deserves no credit. The idea of it was really inspired by the Almighty." This device so increased the plant's productivity that in the fall of 1866 his employers asked him to undertake a general survey of ways to improve their entire operation. He spent several months at the task and turned in a report calling for radical changes in working hours and the pattern of machinery use. In a sense, Muir was one of the first industrial efficiency experts. His suggestions were put into effect and proved highly profitable.

A member of the firm then asked Muir how long he planned to continue working there. "Not long," he said. "Just long enough to earn a few hundred dollars, then I am going on with my studies in the woods." He was told that if he decided to stay, he would be named foreman of the shop, with the promise of a partnership in the company later on. Muir replied that although he liked working with machines and enjoyed the rush and roar of the factory, "Nature's attractions were stronger and I must soon get away."

However, he continued to postpone his departure. Though he had the money he needed, he stayed on into the early months of 1867, becoming more and more deeply involved in the affairs of the wheelmaking company. He thought longingly about the forests, but a career as an industrialist seemed to be taking possession of him. He justified his extended stay in Indianapolis by telling himself that he was creating laborsaving machines to free his fellowmen from drudgery, but what actually held him was that paralysis of the will that had so often afflicted him.

An accident in March, 1867, changed all that. Muir was adjusting the belt of a new saw, using the sharp-pointed end of a file to undo some stitches, when the file slipped and struck him in the eye. "The sight gradually failed," he wrote, "and in a few minutes came perfect darkness. 'My right eye is gone,' I murmured, 'closed forever on all God's beauty.' At first I felt no particular weakness. I walked steadily enough to the house where I was boarding, but in a few hours the shock sent me trembling to bed, and very soon by sympathy the other eye became blind, so that I was in total darkness and feared that I would become permanently blind."

For almost a week he lay in his darkened room, lost in bitterness and despair. "My days were terrible beyond what I can tell, and my nights were if possible more terrible," he declared. "Frightful dreams exhausted and terrified me." A local doctor said his sight was gone, but the Merrills called in a specialist, who examined him carefully and offered an optimistic report. The uninjured eye would regain its full powers as soon as the shock of the accident had diminished, and even the damaged right eye would return to vision in two or three months, though it would never again be perfect.

During his period of recuperation he remained in bed while the young Merrills and their friends came in relays to read to him. As his sight gradually came back, he diverted himself by whittling toys for the children, and he was cheered, too, by the early spring wild flowers that the boys and girls brought him. Also among his visitors were the owners of the factory, who told him that he could take up his position as foreman as soon as he was ready, with a substantial raise in pay; a partnership in the firm would follow in due time. But Muir's narrow escape from blindness had put an end to his career in industry. The world held so much that he longed to see—the jungles of the Amazon Valley, the snow-capped mountains of California, the gleaming glaciers of Alaska—and he had come so close to losing all chance of beholding those wonders! He resolved now to waste no more time inside factories, but to make haste "with all my heart to store my mind with the Lord's beauty and thus be ready for any fate, light or dark." He would set out, once he was fully recovered, on a lifetime of wanderings in the wilderness. "God has to nearly kill us sometimes, to teach us lessons," he observed. But now he "bade adieu to all my mechanical inventions, determined to devote the rest of my life to the study of the inventions of God."

He chose to begin by going south, into the subtropical country along the Gulf of Mexico, now that the terrible Civil War was over. But first he would return to Wisconsin for a last visit with his family. He set out in a leisurely way in the late spring of 1867, botanizing as he went. David and Sarah Galloway now lived at a farm called Mound Hill, near the town of Portage, Wisconsin. While paying a call on them there, Muir discovered on their property a tiny lake hidden in a dense growth of small oaks. It was a gem of a pond, surrounded by a rich growth of ferns, reeds, cattails, and blackberry vines. Fearing that its beauty would be destroyed by the trampling hooves of cattle, Muir asked his brother-in-law to put up a fence to guard Fern Lake from harm. This was perhaps his first attempt at preaching the gospel of conservation, a philosophy that would eventually make him a key figure in the creation of some of the United States' most important national parks. Galloway agreed to fence Fern Lake, but when Muir went on to his family's old Fountain Lake farm and asked its current owner to sell him the acreage around the lake so that it could be preserved as well, the price quoted was too high for him to pay. Fountain Lake went unguarded, and Muir, visiting it again many years later, found the delicate flowers and grasses of the lakeside meadow crushed into black mire by the owner's livestock.

By August Muir was with his parents and sisters at the Hickory Hill farm. It was an unhappy stay. Daniel Muir, now in his sixties, had lost none of his ferocious piety and rasping sense of moral superiority. He rebuked John unceasingly for "walking in the paths of the Devil," telling him in his most stern manner that geology was a blasphemous study, for it contradicted the Bible, and that botany was nearly as wicked. John took most of this abuse meekly, for he had always respected his father's authority no matter how badly the old man provoked him, but when Daniel accused him once too often of godlessness, John finally snapped back, "I'll tell you this, father, I've been spending my time a lot nearer the Almighty than you have!"

There was one further unpleasantness between father and son as John was saying his good-byes to his family. "My son," Daniel asked, "have ye not forgotten something?"

"What have I forgotten, father?"

"Have ye not forgotten to pay for your board and lodging?"

John took out his wallet and frostily gave Daniel a gold piece. Then he said, "Father, you asked me to come home for a visit. I thought I was welcome. You may be very sure it will be a long time before I come again."

He was true to his promise. John Muir saw his father only once again, eighteen years later, when Daniel was on his deathbed.

From Hickory Hill Muir went to Madison to see the Carrs and the Butlers and then back to Indianapolis to bid farewell to the Merrills. On September 1, 1867, he boarded a train that took him across the Ohio River to Louisville, Kentucky. That was as far as he proposed to go by public transportation. "I steered through the big city by compass without speaking a word to anyone," he noted in his journal. "Beyond the city I found a road running southward, and after passing a scatterment of suburban cabins and cottages I reached the green woods and spread out my pocket-map to rough-hew a plan for my journey."

He intended to hike "in a general southward direction by the wildest, leafiest, and least trodden way I could find," down through Kentucky and Tennessee and North Carolina toward Florida's Gulf Coast. There he hoped to board a ship that would take him to South America and the mysterious jungles of the Orinoco and Amazon basins.

Shouldering his pack, he strode away over the oak-covered hills. He tells us that he was "rejoicing in splendid visions of pines and palms and tropic flowers in glorious array"—but not, however, without "a few cold shadows of loneliness."

5

Thousand-Mile Walk to the Gulf

He did not burden himself with excess baggage. All he carried on his southward trek was a small rubber bag containing a comb, towel, brush, change of underclothes, and three small books—the New Testament, the poems of Robert Burns, and Milton's *Paradise Lost.* The bag also held a blank notebook, on the flyleaf of which he had grandly inscribed *"John Muir, Earth-planet, Universe,"* amid a flourish of curlicues.

On the sixth day he reached the cave country of Kentucky and spent a few hours lingering among the ferns at the mouths of several caves, savoring the cold, strong wind that blew up from the earth's depths. He asked a villager how to get to Mammoth Cave, but the man said brusquely that he had no interest in that famous cavern, "as it was nothing but a hole in the ground." Thereafter Muir sought no information from those he encountered, though he greeted everyone with an amiable "Howdy." He hiked all day and slept at night in farmhouses or country taverns. When there was no hospitality to be had, he lay down under a bush or a tree and once entered an empty schoolhouse to sleep "on the softest-looking of the benches."

September 10 saw him beginning the ascent of Tennessee's Cumberland Mountains, "the first real mountains that my foot ever touched or eyes beheld . . . the most sublime . . . picture that ever entered my eyes." But this was country that had been devastated by the Civil War. Most of the farms were deserted, their owners having been killed or driven off. Everything was in ruins. Packs of bandits roved the land, and the few remaining settlers huddled behind locked doors, eyeing all strangers suspiciously. Despite all this, Muir's straightforward way of speaking and openhearted, good-natured approach to people won him lodgings and a meal in many of these poor homes. Even when he came upon ten bandits on horseback, he got past them unharmed with a cheerful smile and a "Howdy." Evidently they thought it would not be worth their while to rob him, but perhaps his fearless attitude made them cautious. He stayed that night with a black family who shared their meal of string beans, buttermilk, and corn bread with him.

By late September he had collected so many plants that he could barely carry his pack. Hunger and thirst had begun to weaken him, and he was suffering now from a low-grade fever. He packed his collections and shipped them to his brother David in Wisconsin, continuing southward, greatly relieved to be rid of the load. But when he entered Georgia early in October, he had a full pack again.

The destruction wrought by the war oppressed him everywhere. He observed the traces of battle "not only on the broken fields, burnt fences, mills, and woods ruthlessly slaughtered, but also on the countenances of the people. A few years after a forest has been burned another generation of bright and happy trees arises, in purest, freshest vigor; only the old trees, wholly or half dead, bear marks of the calamity. So with the people of the war-field. Happy, unscarred, and unclouded youth is growing up around the aged, half-consumed, and fallen parents. . . ." But the recovery from this "most infernal of all civilized calamities" was slow. Roads were shattered; plantation houses were in ruins; coarse rank weeds overran the fields.

In Savannah, Georgia, on October 8, he discovered that money his brother had been supposed to send him had not yet arrived. Feeling "dreadfully lonesome and poor," he went to "the meanest-looking lodging-house that I could find, on account of its cheapness." But he could not afford even that, for he was down to his last dollar and a half, and so he decided to camp outside town until his funds showed up. Four miles from Savannah he discovered an old abandoned graveyard, the Bonaventure Cemetery. It had once been a country estate, and to his delight he found magnificent groves of moss-draped oaks and dense growths of shrubs and ferns. Bald eagles, crows, warblers, many kinds of insects, bright flocks of butterflies—all made the place seem "like a center of life" to him, rather than the realm of the dead. After exploring "one of the most impressive assemblages of animal and plant creatures I ever met," he moved on in search of a place to sleep and soon found himself wandering through a region of dunes where he sank ankle-deep in sand at every step. It seemed like an inhospitable place, full of snakes and unfriendly insects; even the wind had a strange sound. He feared catching malaria there, and also he was concerned about the freed slaves who were wandering menacingly through the district. Where to sleep, then? He thought of the graveyard, where no night prowler bent on banditry would dare to trespass, and hurried back to Bonaventure, reaching it as sunset came.

He strolled for a while through shadowy avenues of trees and then lay down under one of the great oaks, using the mound of a grave for a pillow. The place seemed so beautiful, he wrote, "that almost any sensible person would choose to dwell here with the dead, rather than with the lazy, disorderly living." Buzzing mosquitoes and "large prickly-footed beetles creeping across my hands and face" saw to it, though, that his sleep was "not quite so sound as that of the person below." But he awoke refreshed all the same, and the scenery was so glorious "that hunger and care seemed only a dream."

Each morning Muir walked into Savannah and asked for his money at the post office. Each day the answer was the same: It had not yet come. He would spend the rest of the day wandering around the city, examining the plants in the gardens of the fine homes and town squares, and after dark, when he could not be seen, he returned to his lodgings in the graveyard. He built himself a little bower there, tying the tops of sparkleberry bushes together and covering them with a roof of rushes; a thick bundle of Spanish moss served him as a mattress. In this tiny shelter he slept for five tranquil nights, awakening each morning to the chattering of squirrels and the songs of birds.

He did not neglect his notebook. Finding such peace and beauty in a place reserved for the dead led him to write a brief piece on the follies of society's attitudes toward death. "On no subject," he declared, "are our ideas more warped and pitiable. . . . We are taught that death is an accident, a deplorable punishment for the oldest sin, the arch-enemy of life, etc." We associate it with "groans and tears" and "a black box burial in an ill-omened place, haunted by imaginary glooms and ghosts of every degree." But, he said, "let children walk with Nature, let them see the beautiful blendings and communions of death and life, their joyous inseparable unity, as taught in woods and meadows, plains and mountains and streams . . . and they will learn that death is stingless indeed, and as beautiful as life, and that the grave has no victory, for it never fights. All is divine harmony."

During his stay in Bonaventure Cemetery he lived on nothing but crackers and muddy water. He was suffering fainting fits and, he wrote, "in making the journey to the town was alarmed to find myself growing staggery and giddy. The ground ahead seemed to be rising up in front of me, and the little streams in the ditches on the sides of the road seemed to be flowing up hill. Then I realized that I was becoming dangerously hungry." But at last his money arrived. He rushed with it into the street, bought some gingerbread from a passing vendor, and gobbled it happily. "Thus," he said, "my 'marching through Georgia' terminated handsomely in a jubilee of bread."

Impatient to fulfill his visions of "tropic flowers in glorious array," of "bright-blooming vines and . . . a flood of bright sunshine," he boarded a boat bound for the port of Fernandina on Florida's northern coast. But his first view of Florida was a disappointment: He beheld a vast salt marsh, gloomy and almost impossible to enter. As he sat by the edge of the swamp, lonely and depressed, he heard a sudden noise behind him and felt certain an alligator was about to attack him; he "could feel the stroke of his long notched tail, and could see his big jaws and rows of teeth, closing with a springy snap on me." But he turned to discover that his "man-eating alligator became a tall, white crane, handsome as a minister from spirit land."

The only dry place he could find to walk on in this "watery, vine-tied" land was the embankment of a new railroad line that crossed Florida to Cedar Key on the Gulf of Mexico. Whenever he could, he took side excursions into swamps and pine barrens along his route. His mood varied between exaltation and dejection, with few stages in between. "Night is coming on," he wrote, "and I am filled with indescribable loneliness. Felt feverish; bathed in a black silent stream, nervously watchful for alligators." But on another day he was ecstatic over the unfamiliar plants of this humid wilderness: "The grandest discovery of this great wild day was the palmetto. . . . They tell us that plants are perishable, soulless creatures, that only man is immortal, etc.; but this, I think, is something that we know very nearly nothing about. Anyhow, this palm was indescribably impressive, and told me grander things than I ever got from human priest."

In the port of Cedar Key Muir learned that a local sawmill frequently shipped lumber to Galveston, Texas, by schooner, and he went to the mill to ask if he might take passage on the next vessel to leave. No schooner was due to sail for two weeks, though, and to occupy his time he accepted a temporary job at the mill. But almost at once Muir felt "a strange dullness and headache . . . an inexorable numbness." The fever he had been harboring for several weeks now struck him "like a storm," and he was carried unconscious to the home of the mill owner, a Mr. Hodgson. He wandered in delirium there for days, close to death. Then, slowly, his health began to return under the Hodgsons' devoted care. During his time of convalescence he walked slowly along the shore or drifted in a rowboat among the keys, observing the lush vegetation and the strange tropical birds, pelicans and herons, that screamed at him "with a foreign accent." The Hodgsons insisted he stay as their guest until he was well, and he made use of the opportunity both to further his studies of natural history and to continue his philosophical meditations.

As he sat watching a purple-and-gold sunset from the roof of the Hodgson home, he brooded on the relationship of man and nature. "The world, we are told, was made especially for man—a presumption not supported by all the facts," he wrote. "A numerous class of men are painfully astonished whenever they find anything, living or dead, in all God's universe, which they cannot eat or render in some way what they call useful to themselves." To such men, whales are merely "storehouses of oil for us," hemp was placed on earth only for use in "ship's rigging, wrapping packages, and hanging the wicked," cotton was meant for clothing, iron for hammers and plows, lead for bullets—"all intended for us." But, he wondered, is man really the center of existence? Is he lord of all things? Why, then, "does water drown its lord? Why do so many minerals poison him? Why are so many plants and fishes [his] deadly enemies? Why is the lord of creation subject to the same laws of life as his subjects?"

To Muir, man was merely one creature among many, all of them part of one great harmonious scheme. "The universe would be incomplete without man," he said, "but it would also be incomplete without the smallest transmicroscopic creature that dwells beyond our conceitful eyes and knowledge." He mocked those who, "blind to the rights of all the rest of creation," despised such beasts as alligators and snakes and called them works of the Devil. Alligators, he argued, are "beautiful in the eyes of God," however "fierce and cruel they appear to us." Though such creatures "naturally repel us, they are not mysterious evils. They dwell happily in these flowery wilds, are part of God's family, unfallen, undepraved. . . ." In any conflict between man and nature, Muir preferred to be on the side of nature. No one objected when a "Christian hunter" went to the woods to kill bears and Indians, but let a bear or an Indian kill a hunter and what cries of outrage would arise! The hunter, going forth to slaughter wild animals for sport, liked to say, "They were made for us, for our food, our recreation." But, Muir went on, it was just as reasonable to imagine a bear saying that men were made for bears, "and thanks be to God for claws and teeth so long." He declared that he himself had "precious little sympathy for the selfish propriety of civilized man, and if a war of races should occur between the wild beasts and Lord Man I would be tempted to sympathize with the bears."

In January, 1868, the schooner *Island Belle* called briefly at Cedar Key on her way to Cuba. Muir at once made arrangements to sail with her, over the objections of the Hodgsons, who insisted that he was not yet well. Within a few hours he was on his way. His first day at sea a furious storm arose, and the captain suggested that he go below, but weak and ill though he was, Muir remained on deck, clinging to a rope and thoroughly enjoying the howling of the winds and the surging of the waves.

In Havana he looked about for a ship to take him to Brazil. But he could find none, and he lived aboard the *Island Belle* for a month in the harbor of the Cuban port, spending his days prowling through the coastal swamps and cactus thickets or gathering shells along the coral-encrusted shore. He decided to embark on an exploration of the central mountain range that runs through Cuba from end to end, while waiting for a chance to get to South America. But before he could leave Havana, he was stricken several times with relapses into fever and delirium, and it became clear to him that the disease that had felled him in Florida was malaria. To remain in the tropics, then, would be most unwise. He needed cooler, fresher air. Abruptly he changed his plans and resolved to go to California. Why not? "All the world was before me and every day was a holiday," he said, "so it did not seem important to which one of the world's wildernesses I first should wander."

To get to California Muir first had to go to New York. A schooner loaded with oranges took him there. In the great city he booked steerage passage to San Francisco at a cost of $40 for a three-stage journey: by ship southward from New York to the Isthmus of Panama, by railroad from the Atlantic to the Pacific side of the Isthmus, and by ship again northward from Panama to California. While waiting to embark, he cautiously roamed New York, where he "felt completely lost in the vast throngs of people, the noise of the streets, and the immense size of the buildings. Often I thought I would like to explore the city if, like a lot of wild hills and valleys, it was clear of inhabitants." Many years later he was to say that he had never been as ill at ease on any unknown ice field or gorge as he had been "in these terrible canyons of New York."

He sailed on March 10, 1868. The ship, although small, was jammed with 542 tons of freight and some 400 passengers. "Never had I seen such a barbarous mob, especially at meals," he commented. It was a dismal, uncomfortable journey, with only one cheering moment: the glimpse he had of the jungles of Panama, with a "riotous exuberance of great forest trees, glowing in purple, red, and yellow flowers." On March 28, he landed in San Francisco, a city that he found nearly as ominous and overpowering as New York. Walking up Market Street from the wharf on his first day there, he encountered a carpenter carrying a kit of tools and asked the man where he could find the quickest route out of town. "But where do you want to go?" the carpenter asked. "To any place that is wild," Muir replied. "This reply," he wrote, "startled him. He seemed to fear I might be crazy, and therefore the sooner I was out of town the better, so he directed me to the Oakland ferry."

6

Into the Sierra

Now began one of the most splendid adventures of John Muir's life. Leaving San Francisco hastily behind him, he crossed the bay and set out toward the mountains. He traveled on foot; he carried with him only a blanket and some flour and tea; he had a single companion, a young Englishman named Chilwell whom he had met aboard ship. They headed southward through the Santa Clara Valley as far as the town of Gilroy, then turned eastward toward Pacheco Pass, one of the gateways to the Sierra Nevada range and to the valley known as Yosemite. "It was the bloom-time of the year over the lowlands and coast ranges," Muir wrote. "The landscapes of the Santa Clara Valley were fairly drenched with sunshine, all the air was quivering with the songs of the meadow-larks, and the hills were so covered with flowers that they seemed to be painted."

An even more marvelous sight lay before them as they reached the top of Pacheco Pass. At Muir's feet, 1,500 feet below, lay the Great Central Valley of California, "like a lake of pure sunshine, forty or fifty miles wide, five hundred miles long." It was "a vast level flower garden, smooth and level like a lake of gold—the floweriest part of the world I had yet seen." Looking across to the valley's eastern rim, he beheld through a marvelously clear atmosphere a white wall of mountains, "the mighty Sierra, miles in height, and so gloriously colored and so radiant, it seemed not clothed with light, but wholly composed of it, like the wall of some celestial city."

They went down into the valley, crossed the San Joaquin River by ferry, and began to ascend the Sierra foothills, following the course of the Merced River. At the small mining town of Coulterville they bought provisions and inquired about the trails ahead. A storekeeper told them that the Yosemite trail was still covered in places with 8 or 10 feet of winter snow, which would prevent them from reaching the famous valley for at least a month. He warned them, too, that the mountain forests were full of bears. Neither of these problems troubled Muir, but Chilwell, worried about the bears, insisted on purchasing an old army musket and a few pounds of buckshot.

Up they climbed into the Sierra along the banks of the Merced. As they went higher, the woods changed: groves of oak at a thousand feet; fair-sized pines with large stout cones a little farther up the slopes; then yellow pine becoming more abundant; and, at a height of 6,000 feet, a noble forest of sugar pine, silver fir, Douglas spruce, and the huge, majestic Douglas fir. Heavy snow covered the ground, but it was no obstacle to the two hikers, and Muir rather liked the change from the burning heat of the lowlands. Before long they found themselves on the brow of Yosemite Valley, looking across to Bridal Veil Falls.

The steep granite gorge of Yosemite had been glimpsed by a few explorers in the 1830's and 1840's, but its "official" discovery dates from 1851, when an army battalion chased a band of Indian raiders into the valley. Lafayette Bunnell, a young doctor attached to this battalion, explored the gorge and gave names to many of its most spectacular features, as well as named the valley itself. He called it Yosemite after the name of the Indian tribe that occupied it, a name supposedly meaning "grizzly bear" in their language. By 1855 the first sightseers were touring Yosemite, and in 1864 Congress proclaimed it a public park, setting it aside "for public use, resort and recreation . . . for all time." Since no national park system then existed, the federal government turned the 40-square-mile Yosemite tract over to the State of California to be administered as a state park. The grant included not only the valley itself and its immediate surroundings, but also the Mariposa Grove, a high-lying stand of the giant trees known as sequoias.

Though Yosemite was to be the center of John Muir's life for many years, his first sight of it produced no memorable entries in his journal. Perhaps he found it too grand to capture in words. He merely tells us that he and Chilwell spent "eight or ten days in visiting the falls and the high points of view around the walls, making sketches, collecting flowers and ferns, etc." Then they decided to return to the lowlands, going by way of the Mariposa sequoias. On the eve of their departure from the valley, as they ate supper by the light of their campfire, they had their first meeting with a Yosemite bear. A heavy crackling of twigs told them of his approach: a brown bear coming up on the opposite side of the fire, 25 or 30 feet away. Chilwell, alarmed, handed the gun to Muir—he had no idea how to use one himself—and both men sat hushed and motionless, waiting to see what the bear would do. "Finally, after sniffing and whining for his supper what seemed to us a long time," Muir wrote, "the young inexperienced beast walked off. We were much afraid of his return to attack us. We did not then know that bears never attack sleeping campers, and dreading another visit we kept awake on guard most of the night."

A few days later, after moving without difficulty over the snow-choked trails, they came to the outpost called Wawona. A pioneer named Galen Clark lived there, serving as the state's guardian of the park, keeping watch against trespassers and timber cutters. Clark let them have some flour and also a piece of bear meat. They had lived on nothing but bread and tea for many days, and Chilwell devoured the meat eagerly, though to Muir "it seemed so rank and oily that I was unable to swallow a single morsel."

Soon they were among the gigantic sequoias of Mariposa—some of the biggest trees on earth, trees bigger than Muir had imagined it was possible for trees to be. Many of them reached heights above 250 feet. More than 200 of the trees in the grove were at least 10 feet thick at the base; some had diameters of 25 or 30 feet, wider than a highway. "We camped here long uncounted days," Muir reported, "wandering about from tree to tree, taking no note of time. The longer we gazed the more we admired not only their colossal size, but their majestic beauty and dignity. Greatest of trees, greatest of living things, their noble domes poised in unchanging repose seemed to belong to the sky, while the great firs and pines about them looked like mere latter-day saplings."

After more than a month in the Yosemite region, Muir and Chilwell descended to the hot San Joaquin plain. Their money was nearly gone, though the total cost of their uplands journey had been only $3 each, and since the grain of the lowland farms was almost ripe, they took jobs as harvesters. Writing to his brother David, Muir said that the mountains, "together with the purple plains and pure sky," form "a source of exhaustless and unmeasurable happiness from all the fields where I work. Farming was a grim, material, debasing pursuit under Father's generalship. But I think much more favorably of it now." Chilwell drifted away after the harvest was in, but Muir stayed on, breaking mustang horses for a rancher and operating a ferry at Merced Falls. He was saving money so that he could return to the Sierra for a longer and more far-reaching trip.

In the autumn of 1868 Muir worked for a while shearing sheep for a San Joaquin Valley rancher. When the shearing was over, he was offered a job as a shepherd, and though he insisted he knew nothing about caring for sheep, he let himself be hired for the winter at a salary of $30 a month plus board. The job, he decided, would enable him to be out of doors every day, studying the birds and beasts and plants of the plain while he looked after his flock. Late in the year he settled down with two trained sheep dogs and 1,800 sheep on a grazing range about two miles from the town of Snelling.

The cabin in which he had to live, he said, was "worse than a Hottentot's hut." Every yard of its floor was strewn with debris left behind by previous shepherds—"bits of shriveled woolly skin, bacon rinds, bones, horns and skulls mixed with all sorts of mysterious compound unclean rubbish!" Wild hogs roamed about, contributing to the disorder. On his first morning at the job he opened the gate of the corral and let the flock come forth "like a boisterous uncontrollable flood," and soon the sheep were scattered so widely over the plain that "it seemed impossible that the mad starving creatures could ever be got together again." He ran around wildly, trying to keep the animals within an area of about a square mile. About noon, to his surprise, "they lay down to rest and allowed me to do the same for an hour or so. Then they again scattered, but not so far nor so wildly, and I was still more surprised about half an hour before sundown, while I was wondering how I could ever get them driven back into the corral, to see them gather of their own accord into long parallel files, across Dry Creek on the bank of which the corral stood, and pour back into the corral and quietly lie down. This ended my first-day of sheep-herding." Muir never lost his disdain for the stupidity and timidity of sheep. "Sheep brain must surely be poor stuff," he wrote. "A sheep can hardly be called an animal; an entire flock is required to make one foolish individual." He admired the wild sheep of the mountains immensely, but it seemed to him that these placid tame beasts of the corral had been drained of all vitality and intelligence by man's influence.

Five months passed in this fashion. The sheep were dull companions, but there was the excitement of watching the parched plain come to life once the winter rains set in, in mid-December. Dry Creek became a deep, stately flowing river, and lush grass three or four inches high sprang up where there had been only dust and dead stems. Suddenly mosses and liverworts "covered the entire plain with a soft velvet robe of living green. Then, at first one by one, the different species of flowering plants appeared, pushing up with marvelous rapidity and bursting into bloom." When the cold rainy season was past, ants and other insects came forth from "their deathlike sleep," and ground squirrels emerged from the burrows to sun themselves and feed on the new plants. Jackrabbits scampered over the plain. "Several times," Muir wrote, "I saw inquisitive sheep interviewing the rabbits as they sat erect, even touching noses and indulging apparently in interesting gossip." Eagles soared high above, waiting to seize some unwary rabbit far from its burrow. The spring also brought hundreds of "little, thick-legged, wrinkled duplicates—unhappy lambs born to wretchedness and unmitigated degradation." They provided more work for him; when a late frost struck, he wandered over the hills in driving sleet, rounding up the lambs and carrying them to his cabin. At one point some 200 woolly babies clustered in the hut; he thawed them by a blazing fire, fed them milk from a bottle, and saved the lives of most of them.

Summer came rushing on. The green beauty of April gave way to the fierce heat of May, when the flowers of the plain went to seed and died, and the grass, scorched and sun-dried, crumbled underfoot as if baked in an oven. It was time to lead the sheep toward the cool, lofty pastures of the Sierra, driving them higher and higher as the snows melted and the summer swept up the slopes. Muir did not expect to be taking them there, for he had been hired only as a winter shepherd. But he was planning to head for the high Sierra himself. His health was fully restored—he had chased the fevers of malaria with mountain winds and crystal water—and he was hungry for a longer look at the wonders he had glimpsed in the spring of 1868. But he was not sure how he could carry enough food into the high country to last him for a whole summer or where he would camp.

At this point a rancher named Pat Delaney, for whom Muir had worked as a sheep shearer the previous fall, came to his aid. Delaney, an educated man who had studied for the priesthood, was aware of Muir's botanical interests and had looked with pleasure through Muir's drawings of unusual plants. Now he urged Muir to go to the mountains with his flock for the summer—"not to herd the sheep, for the regular shepherd was to take care of them, but simply to see that the shepherd did his duties. He offered to carry my plant press and blankets, allow me to make his mountain camps my headquarters while I was studying the adjacent mountains, and perfect freedom to pursue my studies, and offering to pay me besides, simply to see that the shepherd did not neglect his flock."

It was a perfect opportunity, for the sheep were due to go to the headwaters of the Merced and Tuolumne rivers—the very region Muir had most in mind. He protested mildly that he did not know the mountain country and would be of little practical use, but Delaney easily talked him into accepting the offer. On June 3, 1869, Muir set out on the jaunt that would give him the material for one of his most famous books, *My First Summer in the Sierra.* "This morning," he wrote, "provisions, campkettles, blankets, plant-press, etc., were packed on two horses, the flock headed for the tawny foothills, and away we sauntered in a cloud of dust: Mr. Delaney, bony and tall, with sharply hacked profile like Don Quixote, leading the pack-horses, Billy, the proud shepherd, a Chinaman and a Digger Indian to assist in driving for the first few days in the brushy foothills, and myself with notebook tied to my belt."

In five days the dusty foothills were behind them, and they were camped in a picturesque hollow on the north fork of the Merced River. "How deep our sleep last night in the mountain's heart," Muir wrote on June 9, "beneath the trees and stars, hushed by solemn-sounding waterfalls and many small soothing voices in sweet accord whispering peace! And our first pure mountain day, warm, calm, cloudless—how immeasurable it seems, how serenely wild!" The work of spring was going on everywhere, "new life, new beauty, unfolding, unrolling in glorious exuberant extravagance." Muir observed the most minute details: a colony of jet-black ants tunneling through a huge dead pine, a cluster of brilliant-hued lizards darting about on sun-warmed rocks, a curious twining lily climbing the branches of poison oak. He studied the way fast-flowing streams pile boulders into dams and then sweep the dams away. He measured the foot-long needles of the yellow pine and collected its cones. One day the observer found himself the observed, when an Indian wandered into the camp: "I was seated on a stone, looking over my notes and sketches, and happening to look up, was startled to see him standing grim and silent within a few steps of me, as motionless and weather-stained as an old tree-stump that had stood there for centuries.

All Indians seem to have learned this wonderful way of walking unseen—making themselves invisible like certain spiders I have been observing here. . . ."

The surface of the mountains seemed "smooth and changeless" to him, very different from that of the lower valleys, where gold miners had blasted roads in the solid rock, had dammed and tamed wild streams, had left scars of excavation and construction all over the landscape. But nature's scars were there to be seen as well. On July 10, when they were camped on Tamarack Creek just above the Merced Canyon, Muir left the camp and turned his magnifying glass on the deep scratches he saw in great granite boulders. He remembered his glacial studies of university days; surely those scratches were the work of ancient rivers of ice. And how had these boulders come to be here in the first place? "With what tool were they quarried and carried?" he asked himself. A glacier, yes, a glacier flowing down from the northeast, he supposed, "grinding down the general mass of the mountains. . . . A FINE DISCOVERY THIS!"

At one stage of the march they ran out of flour. This was a great hardship for Muir, who disliked meat and preferred to eat hard bread or oatmeal cakes on his mountain journeys. Plenty of mutton was available, and tea and sugar, but without bread Muir found himself "weak and sickish. . . . Can scarce command attention to my best studies." He found, after a week of a breadless diet, that his stomach was restless and he could not swallow the mutton without nausea. "Just bread and water and delightful toil is all I need," he wrote. Finally Delaney, who had gone back to the lowlands, reappeared with a fresh supply of flour, and Muir's bread famine was ended.

Now they went "climbing toward cloudland." As they ascended, the forest grew ever more beautiful, and Muir was dismayed by the destruction caused by Delaney's 2,050 sheep. They trampled leaves and flowers and stripped the bushes bare; Muir bitterly called the animals "hooved locusts" that left fearful devastation as they passed. They reached a marshy meadow where lilies grew, seven to eight feet high with splendid clusters of orange-colored flowers. "And to think," he wrote, "that the sheep should be allowed in these lily meadows! after how many centuries of Nature's care planting and watering them, tucking the bulbs in snugly below winter frost, shading the tender shoots with clouds drawn above them like curtains, pouring refreshing rain, making them perfect in beauty, and keeping them safe by a thousand miracles. . . . As far as I have seen, man alone, and the animals he tames, destroy these gardens."

Then they met a party of tourists, mounted on mules and ponies: "A strange show they made, winding single file through the solemn woods in gaudy attire, scaring the wild creatures, and one might fancy that even the great pines would be disturbed and grown aghast. But what may we say of ourselves and the flock?"

July 15 saw them camped on the edge of the Yosemite Valley. After lunch he hurried up a ridge to the highest point he could find. "Nearly all the upper basin of the Merced was displayed, with its sublime domes and canyons, dark upsweeping forests, and glorious array of white peaks deep in the sky, every feature glowing, radiating beauty that pours into our flesh and bones like heat rays from fire," he wrote. "Sunshine over all; no breath of wind to stir the brooding calm." In his ecstasy he shouted and waved his arms so wildly that one of the sheep dogs, a St. Bernard, came running up to him with a look of "puzzled concern" in his eyes, and a brown bear that happened to be prowling in a nearby thicket ran away as though he considered Muir dangerous, "tumbling over the tops of the tangled Manzanita bushes in his haste."

Leaving the others, Muir walked southward until the valley itself was in view. He stared in awe at its towering walls, "sculptured into endless variety of domes and gables, spires and precipices," and at the enormous Half Dome at the valley's upper end, rising almost a mile high, "the most impressive of all the rocks." He crept out to the brink of the valley, where he could look clear down the face of the wall to the bottom. "I could not help fearing a little that the rock might split off and let me down, and what a down!—more than three thousand feet. Still my limbs did not tremble, nor did I feel the least uncertainty as to the reliance to be placed on them." After a mile of precarious crawling along the cliff, he came to the place where Yosemite Creek leaps into space to become Yosemite Falls. "Emerging from its last gorge, it glides in wide lace-like rapids down a smooth incline into a pool where it seems to rest and compose its gray, agitated waters before taking the grand plunge, then slowly slipping over the lip of the pool basin, it descends another glossy slope with rapidly accelerated speed to the brink of the tremendous cliff, and with sublime, fateful confidence springs out free in the air."

He removed his shoes and stockings and worked his way out to the edge of the ridge over which the waterfall tumbles, hoping to be able to lean far enough over to see the course of the fall all the way to the bottom. But one final brow of rock blocked his view. Studying it, he "discovered a narrow shelf about three inches wide on the very brink, just wide enough for a rest for one's heels." He realized that to try to reach it was unreasonably risky, yet he found himself making the attempt anyway, filling his mouth with the leaves of a bitter weed, "hoping they might help to prevent giddiness." He reached the little ledge safely, planted his heels on it, and shuffled sideways 20 or 30 feet until he could look directly "down into the heart of the snowy, chanting throng of comet-like streamers, into which the body of the fall soon separates. While perched on that narrow niche I was not distinctly conscious of danger. The tremendous grandeur of the fall in form and sound and motion, acting at close range, smothered the sense of fear. . . . How long I remained down there, or how I returned, I can hardly tell." He promised himself that "hereafter I'll try to keep from such extravagant, nerve-straining places," but he must have known it was a promise that would be broken many times.

Now began six joyous weeks of adventure in the high country above Yosemite. Everything was a source of wonder. A rainstorm came "with keen startling thunder, the metallic, ringing, clashing, clanging notes gradually fading into low bass rolling and muttering in the distance." Daybreak and sunrise were studies in rich color: "The pale rose and purple sky changing softly to daffodil yellow and white, sunbeams pouring through the passes between the peaks and over the Yosemite domes, making their edges burn. . . ." A common housefly and a grasshopper paid him "a merry visit" as he sat sketching atop Half Dome; he took delight in the grasshopper's "glad, hilarious energy" and wondered what had drawn the housefly, so "fond of domestic ease," this far up the mountains. A bear visited him there also, and Muir examined him coolly, "noting the sharp muzzle thrust inquiringly forward, the long shaggy hair on his broad chest, the stiff erect ears nearly buried in hair, and the slow heavy way he moved his head." They stared at each other a long while before the bear walked away, "evidently neither fearing me very much nor trusting me." Those were magical weeks: "No pain here, no dull empty hours, no fear of the past, no fear of the future. . . . I gaze and sketch and bask. . . ." But to his companion, the shepherd Billy, Yosemite was "but a canyon—a lot of rocks—a hole in the ground—a place dangerous about falling into—a damned good place to keep away from."

Late in July Muir climbed to the summit of Mount Hoffman, 11,000 feet above sea level, his highest point yet. There he found the beautiful mountain hemlock with its drooping branches in full bloom and the strange, stunted dwarf pine of the timberline. There, too, he studied the gouges and basins the glaciers had carved. Then he descended by way of Lake Tenaya, where he entered a forest of silver fir and measured one tree at 240 feet in height. By August 2 he was back at the domes overlooking Yosemite, and that afternoon, while sketching on North Dome, he had a curious experience: He was "suddenly, without warning, possessed with the notion that my friend, Professor J. D. Butler, of the State University of Wisconsin, was below me in the valley, and I jumped up full of the idea of meeting him." Without questioning the impulse, Muir instantly started to scramble down the side of the canyon into the valley "as if drawn irresistibly." But then he reflected that he would arrive after dark at the hotel down there, coatless and wearing grubby, ragged clothes. So he forced himself to halt and go to his camp. In the morning, though, dressed in "a clean pair of overalls, a cashmere shirt, and a sort of jacket—the best my camp wardrobe afforded," he made his way into the valley. Tourists at the hotel stared at him "in silent wonderment, as if I had been seen dropping down through the trees from the clouds." He asked at the desk for Professor Butler. Yes, he was told, a Professor Butler had arrived the day before and was now hiking in the valley. Muir rushed off, running four miles to Vernal Falls and finding Butler "as the compass-needle finds the pole." The professor, unaware that Muir was in Yosemite, did not recognize him at first; then he cried out, "John Muir, John Muir, where have you come from?" Muir explained the story of "last evening's telepathy, transcendental revelation, or whatever else it may be called." It was the first of three such adventures in telepathy he was to have.

Muir stayed in the valley that night. "It seemed strange," he wrote, "to sleep in a paltry hotel chamber after the spacious magnificence of the starry sky." After a long gossipy talk with his old friend, he scrambled toward his mountain home, pitying all those who were "bound by clocks, almanacs, orders, duties, etc., and compelled to dwell with lowland care and dust and din . . . while the poor, insignificant wanderer enjoys the freedom and glory of God's wilderness." He poured into his notebook his contempt for the tourists he had seen in the valley, who were "so little influenced by its novel grandeur, as if their eyes were bandaged and their ears stopped. Most of those I saw yesterday were looking down as if wholly unconscious of anything going on about them, while the sublime rocks were trembling with the tones of the mighty chanting congregation of waters gathered from all the mountains round about, making music that might draw angels out of heaven."

Bears now were raiding the corral. They killed only a few sheep, but others died when they piled up against the side of the corral in fright and suffocated. Pat Delaney, learning of the losses, ordered his shepherd to break camp and take the flock to the safety of the high grassy forests north of the Tuolumne Meadows. On August 7 they began the slow march eastward along the Mono Trail. The next day, camping beside Lake Tenaya, Muir "took a walk on the glacier-polished pavements along the north shore, and climbed the magnificent mountain rock at the east end of the lake. . . . Almost every yard of its surface shows the scoring and polishing action of a great glacier that enveloped it and swept heavily over its summit, though it is about two thousand feet high above the lake and ten thousand above sea level. This majestic, ancient ice-flood came from the eastward, as the scoring and crushing of the surface shows. . . . In climbing the steepest polished places I had to take off shoes and stockings. A fine region this for study of glacial action in mountain-making. . . ." All along the trail he saw the same signs: "This entire region," he concluded, "must have been overswept by ice."

Ahead of the sheep he reached the "flowery lawns" of the Tuolumne Meadows and went on a long ramble, enjoying the fine, silky grass, the clouds of purple blossoms, and the crystal-clear glacier-carved lakes, populated by frogs "in hearty health and voice. I like their cheery tronk and crink. They take the place of songbirds at a pinch." He roamed "from meadow to meadow, every one beautiful beyond telling," and wrote in despair, "To let sheep trample so fine a place seems barbarous."

They remained at the Tuolumne camp for a month. Muir climbed many of the highest peaks, adding to his store of glacial knowledge. Also he went eastward through Bloody Canyon and down to the edge of the Mono Desert on the far side of the Sierra and gloried in the contrasts: "Hot deserts bounded by snow-laden mountains—cinders and ashes scattered on glacier-polished pavements—frost and fire working together in the making of beauty." Returning from that torrid plain to the cool, snow-spangled mountains, Muir felt that his sense of nature's variety and underlying harmony had been immeasurably deepened. "When we try to pick out anything by itself, we find it hitched to everything else in the universe," he wrote. "The whole wilderness in unity and interrelation is alive and familiar." And he was aware now of the constant motion, the eternal pulsing, of the natural world, as this lyrical passage from his notebook shows:

"Contemplating the lace-like fabric of streams outspread over the mountains, we are reminded that everything is flowing—going somewhere, animals and so-called lifeless rocks as well as water. Thus the snow flows fast or slow in grand beauty-making glaciers and avalanches; the air in majestic floods carrying minerals, plant leaves, seeds, spores, with streams of music and fragrance; water streams carrying rocks both in solution and in form of mud particles, sand, pebbles, and boulders. Rocks flow from volcanoes like water from springs, and animals flock together and flow in currents modified by stepping, leaping, gliding, flying, swimming, etc. While the stars go streaming through space pulsed on and on forever like blood globules in Nature's warm heart."

At the end of August the first frosts touched the Sierra meadows. It was time to return to the lowlands. Muir was reluctant to go. "If I had a few sacks of flour, an axe, and some matches," he wrote, "I would build a cabin of pine logs, pile up plenty of firewood about it and stay all winter to see the grand fertile snow-storms, watch the birds and animals that winter thus high, how they live, how the forests look snow-laden or buried, and how the avalanches look and sound on their way down the mountains. But now I'll have to go, for there is nothing to spare in the way of provisions. I'll surely be back, however, surely I'll be back. No other place has ever so overwhelmingly attracted me as this hospitable, Godful wilderness." Ripe pine cones were falling; autumn colors tinged the trees and meadows. On September 9 the retreat began. "May the good time come when I can stay as long as I like with plenty of bread, far and free from trampling flocks. . . ." Down toward the lowlands trotted the sheep, and down with them came John Muir, pausing, turning back for one last look, and closing his journal with the words "I have crossed the Range of Light, surely the brightest and best of all the Lord has built; and rejoicing in its glory, I gladly, gratefully, hopefully pray I may see it again."

7

The Mountain Years

The splendor of the mountains had touched the core of John Muir's soul; he could not now remain long in the lowlands. For eight weeks in the autumn of 1869 he worked on the Delaney ranch, receiving there the agreeable news that his Wisconsin friend Dr. Ezra Slocum Carr had obtained a professorship at the University of California. The Carrs now were living in Oakland, and Mrs. Carr wrote to Muir, inviting him to stay with them. He replied on November 15, 1869, that he would gladly "enjoy a blink of rest in your new home, [but] I must return to the mountains—to Yosemite. I am told that the winter storms there will not be easily borne, but I am bewitched, enchanted, and tomorrow I must start for the great temple to listen to the winter songs and sermons preached and sung only there."

Accompanied by Harry Randall, a young Philadelphian who had been working at the Delaney ranch, Muir trudged to Yosemite and presented himself at the Hutchings Hotel in the valley, looking for a winter job. The landlord there was a tall, lean Englishman named James M. Hutchings, who had come to California the same year Muir had crossed the Atlantic from Scotland. In 1855 he had begun to publish the *Illustrated California Magazine,* which frequently ran articles extolling the beauties of the Yosemite region. Chiefly as a result of these pieces, tourists began to enter the valley, and two small hotels were built in it in the days before it became a public park. Hutchings himself purchased the larger of these hotels, opposite Yosemite Falls, in 1859. When the park legislation was passed five years later, he embarked on a ten-year lawsuit to keep his land.

Though his case was still moving through the courts in 1869, Hutchings had decided to expand his hotel and was looking for someone to design, build, and operate a sawmill to supply lumber for this project. Muir's past experience made him the perfect man for the assignment. At first glance it may seem odd to find a conservationist like John Muir agreeing to run a sawmill in the heart of Yosemite Park, but before he accepted the job, he made certain that Hutchings had no plans for cutting down living trees, which would have been a violation of the park's sanctity. Hutchings had no such intentions. A storm in 1867 had blown down more than a hundred immense pines, and all the timber he could possibly need was lying on the ground waiting to be used.

So Muir had a job for the winter. Deep snows already mantled the meadows and clothed Half Dome in white; with delight he witnessed the "booming, out-bounding avalanches," "the coming and going of the noble storms," and "the growth of frost crystals on the rocks and leaves and snow." His first task was to build a cabin for himself on the north side of the valley. Its walls were of rough pine shingles, and its floor was fashioned from flat slabs of stone out of Yosemite Creek. He dug a ditch that brought a stream into the cabin, "entering at one end and flowing out the other with just current enough to allow it to sing and warble in low, sweet tones, delightful at night while I lay in bed." There was one window, facing Yosemite Falls; he slept in a hammock giving him a view of that great cascade. He provided himself with a bookcase, a table, a bench, a writing desk, and two chairs. In the spring ferns sprouted between the floor slabs; he trained them to grow up the wall and around the window in front of his desk. Frogs came in with the stream, climbing the ferns and making "fine music in the night." The entire cost of the cabin, which he called "the handsomest building in the valley," was less than $4.

Then he set up the sawmill and went to work cutting up the fallen trees. When enough lumber was on hand, he and two carpenters renovated the main hotel building and constructed outlying cottages. By late April the snows were melting and everything was in readiness for the season's first crop of tourists. Since Hutchings was away in Washington fighting his legal battles, Muir found himself required to serve as a guide, which was not at all to his liking. "All sorts of human stuff is being poured into our valley this year," he wrote to Mrs. Carr in May, 1870, "and the blank, fleshly apathy with which most of it comes in contact with the rock and water spirits of the place is most amazing." He described them climbing sprawlingly into their saddles "like overgrown frogs" and touring the valley "with about as much emotion as the horses they ride upon," while longing for "the safety and flatness of their proper homes." Still, Muir did not share Mrs. Carr's fears that tourists would desecrate Yosemite. He believed that "the tide of visitors will float slowly about the *bottom* of the valley as a harmless scum collecting in hotel and saloon eddies, leaving the rocks and falls eloquent as ever." It was the top of the valley, "more than halfway to real heaven," where he would go in solitude. "I am very, very blessed," he said. "The valley is full of people, but they do not annoy me. I revolve in pathless places and in higher rocks than *the world* and his ribbony wife can reach."

Many of the tourists arrived bearing copies of *The Yosemite Guide Book,* written by Josiah D. Whitney, professor of geology at Harvard and state geologist of California. In this popular book Whitney, one of the most respected geologists of his day, offered an explanation of how Yosemite Valley had been formed. What had happened, he said, was that a violent earthquake in ancient times had torn the region apart. In places the land had been thrust upward, forming the great peaks of the Sierra Nevada; in other places it "sank down to an unknown depth, owing to its support being withdrawn from underneath, during some of those convulsive movements which must have attended the upheaval of so extensive and elevated a chain." To Whitney the creation of Yosemite was entirely due to this titanic cataclysm. In 1865 a geologist named Clarence King, noticing the same gouges and scratches Muir would see a few years later, had suggested that the erosive action of glaciers might have carved the valley. "A more absurd theory was never advanced," Whitney declared in 1868. "This theory based on entire ignorance of the whole subject may be dropped without wasting any more time upon it."

Now here was John Muir, this wild-looking, shaggy-bearded man in ragged clothes, also telling people that glaciers, not earthquakes, had created Yosemite. "Whitney says that the bottom has fallen out of the rocks here—which I most devoutly disbelieve," he wrote Mrs. Carr in April, 1870. According to Whitney, Half Dome and other flat-faced Yosemite mountains had been "split asunder" by "the wreck of matter and the crash of worlds," but Muir insisted to the tourists that they had been cleft by mighty rivers of ice. "I can take you where you can see for yourself," he cried, "how the glaciers have labored, and cut and carved, and elaborated, until they have wrought out this royal road." Most of his listeners assumed he was a crank and clung to Whitney's theory. A few, caught up in Muir's eloquence, actually went to look at the glacial marks, and came away converted. Whitney himself, learning of Muir's beliefs, called him "a mere sheep-herder" and "an ignoramus," and dismissed his ideas scornfully.

In August, 1870, Joseph Le Conte, professor of geology at the University of California, brought nine students on a field trip to Yosemite. Le Conte, a pupil of the great glacier expert Louis Agassiz, had heard about Muir from the Carrs, and sought him out. He was, Le Conte wrote, "a man in rough miller's garb, whose intelligent face and earnest clear blue eyes excited my interest." Le Conte listened sympathetically to Muir's talk of glacial action and invited him to come along on a ten-day expedition across the mountains to Mono Lake. Camping at Eagle Point, overlooking the valley on the north side, Muir pointed out to Le Conte the route by which he thought the glaciers had come and indicated the various cleavages and tracks that demonstrated their onetime presence. That night Le Conte noted in his journal, "I strongly incline to the belief that a glacier once filled the Yosemite." He differed with Muir in one respect, for he felt that water had eroded the Sierra canyons to some degree before the arrival of the glaciers—a point in which modern research has proved him correct—but generally he agreed with Muir's concepts. Le Conte was the first important scientist to give his support to Muir. "He is really not only an intelligent man, as I saw at once," Le Conte wrote, "but a man of strong, earnest nature, and thoughtful, closely observing and original mind." But for the time being Muir was in no position to challenge the teachings of the prestigious Josiah Whitney.

In the fall of 1870, after a long and tiresome summer guiding chattering tourists along the valley trails, Muir abruptly left Yosemite. He had had too little time to himself all season, although it had seemed to James Hutchings that he had had too much; his employer had grumbled that Muir "just wouldn't attend to business, but wandered about studying wild flowers." Hutchings' apparent jealousy of Muir's great popularity among the tourists he guided was another source of friction between them. Quitting in disgust, Muir hiked to the lowlands by way of Merced Canyon and several extraordinary groves of giant sequoias and took a temporary job again on Pat Delaney's ranch. There he received a letter from Mrs. Carr, inviting him to join an expedition to the upper Amazon, but though he had never abandoned his dream of exploring South America, Muir declined, saying that he felt he still had more to see in the Sierra Nevada.

In January, 1871, he returned to Yosemite, peaceful now under winter's snows. Despite their disagreements, Hutchings rehired him to run the sawmill. Hutchings' sister now was living in the cabin Muir had built, so he built a new one for himself, "a small box-like home fastened beneath the gable of the mill," high above the ground—"a hang-bird's hang-nest," he called it. With this as his base he wandered through the snowy forests, heedless of the weather. During these quiet winter hours he thought a good deal about himself, his restlessness, his love of solitude. He was almost thirty-three years old, a bachelor, a wanderer, a man without a profession. All the members of his family were "useful members of society—save me." All were "exemplary, stable, anti-revolutionary"—except John Muir. But surely, since the Muirs had contributed so many diligent citizens to the workaday world, he could be spared for the experiment of a life in the wilderness. And so he attempted to banish all guilt over the role he had chosen. "I will follow my instincts, be myself for good or ill, and see what will be the upshot," he resolved. "As long as I live, I'll hear waterfalls and birds and winds sing. I'll interpret the rocks, learn the language of flood, storm, and the avalanche. I'll acquaint myself with the glaciers and wild gardens, and get as near the heart of the world as I can."

To get near the heart of the world, also, there came to Yosemite in the spring of 1871 the revered New England sage, one of Muir's idols, Ralph Waldo Emerson. The great philosopher, sixty-eight years old, was on a long Western trip and planned to spend a few days in the celebrated valley. To Muir's disappointment, Emerson and his entourage took accommodations not at the Hutchings Hotel but at its rival establishment, Leidig's, farther downstream opposite Sentinel Rock. Muir went down there for a glimpse of the famous man, whose books he had studied with such care. "I was excited as I had never been excited before," Muir said many years later, "and my heart throbbed as if an angel direct from heaven had alighted on the Sierran rocks. But so great was my awe and reverence, I did not dare to go to him or speak to him. I hovered on the outside of the crowd of people that were pressing forward to be introduced to him and shaking hands with him."

But when Muir learned that Emerson meant to remain in Yosemite only a short while, desperation gave him courage, and he sent a note to Emerson's hotel, telling him that to leave so soon was an injustice to the wonders of the valley. Something in Muir's fervent words caught Emerson's interest, and the next morning he rode up to the sawmill to have a look at the man who had written that passionate message. It was a marvelous moment for John Muir. In 1836, two years before his birth, Emerson had published a small book called *Nature,* a romantic, idealistic, almost revolutionary volume urging man to enter into harmony with his environment. Through all his adult life Muir had guided himself by Emerson's principles. And now here was Emerson himself, come to call on him!

Fighting back his shyness, Muir invited Emerson into the "hang-nest." Bravely scrambling up "a series of sloping planks roughened by slats like a hen ladder," the old man entered Muir's eyrie and looked through his collections of dried plants and flowers, mineral specimens, and sketches of mountains, trees, and glacial lakes. "He seemed as serene as a sequoia," Muir wrote. "Forgetting his age, plans, duties, ties of every sort, I proposed an immeasurable camping trip back in the heart of the mountains." Emerson seemed eager to accept, but he was traveling with a group of friends and disciples from Boston, bookish, inactive men all, who would not hear of letting their fragile mentor venture into the rough wilderness. "Alas," Muir wrote, "it was too late—too near the sundown of his life. The shadows were growing long, and he leaned on his friends. His party, full of indoor philosophy, failed to see the natural beauty . . . of my wild plan, and laughed at it in good-natured ignorance. . . . Anyhow, they would have none of it, and held Mr. Emerson to the hotels and trails."

Muir did see Emerson every day for the rest of his five days in the valley. Though one of Emerson's companions spoke condescendingly of Muir's "amusing zeal," Emerson took no such lofty attitude, and listened with evident interest to Muir's stories of the mountains. For Muir, it was a chance to pour out his soul to the one man in all the world most likely to understand his own dreams and longings, and he seized his opportunity. When Emerson left Yosemite, he invited Muir to accompany his group as far as the Mariposa sequoias. Muir agreed, on the condition that Emerson would camp out with him one night in the grove. "Yes, yes, we will camp out," Emerson said. But Muir was due for another disappointment. "Early in the afternoon," he wrote, "when we reached Clark's Station [at Wawona], I was surprised to see the party dismount. And when I asked if we were not going up into the grove to camp they said: 'No, it would never do to lie out in the night air. Mr. Emerson might take cold; and you know, Mr. Muir, that would be a dreadful thing.' In vain I urged, that only in homes and hotels were colds caught, that nobody ever was known to take cold camping in these woods, that there was not a single cough or sneeze in all the Sierra. Then I pictured the big climate-changing, inspiring fire I would make, praised the beauty and fragrance of sequoia flame, told how the great trees would stand about us transfigured in purple light. . . . But the house habit was not to be overcome, nor the strange dread of pure night air." Off they went to "the carpet dust and unknowable reeks" of Galen Clark's hotel.

The next day they rode on into the grove "and stayed an hour or two, mostly in ordinary tourist fashion—looking at the biggest giants, measuring them with a tape line, riding through prostrate fire-bored trunks, etc., though Mr. Emerson was alone occasionally, sauntering about as if under a spell." The time was soon gone, but Muir made one last attempt to get Emerson to remain. "You are yourself a sequoia," he said. "Stop and get acquainted with your big brethren." Nevertheless, Emerson's "affectionate but sadly civilized friends" took him away. Muir followed them to the edge of the grove. Emerson lingered behind the others, and, Muir wrote, "when he reached the top of the ridge, after all the rest of the party were over and out of sight, he turned his horse, took off his hat and waved me a last goodbye. I felt lonely, so sure I had been that Emerson of all men would be the quickest to see the mountains and sing them." He wandered back alone into the grove and made a bed for himself of fallen branches and ferns. "After sundown I built a great fire, and as usual had it all to myself. And though lonesome for the first time in these forests, I quickly took heart again—the trees had not gone to Boston, nor the birds; and as I sat by the fire, Emerson was still with me in spirit, though I never again saw him in the flesh."

Emerson's way home took him through Oakland, where he visited Dr. and Mrs. Ezra Slocum Carr and spoke at length of the pleasure his too-brief visit with Muir had given him. "I have laid up in my heart so much that he told me," Mrs. Carr wrote to Muir. "I wait to talk with you about it. . . ." Emerson would live another eleven years. He sent occasional letters and packages of books to Muir, and received from him, now and then, twigs and dried blossoms to remind him of his days in Yosemite. A few years after Emerson's death, the naturalist John Burroughs, browsing through his journals, discovered a short list of the great men Emerson had known. The last name on the list, added at the close of Emerson's life, was that of John Muir.

The problem of the origin of Yosemite concerned Muir ever more deeply in 1871. He was convinced that Whitney's theory of the valley's formation in an earthquake was wrong and that his own notion that glaciers had carved it was correct. But he needed more proof before he could seriously challenge a man of Whitney's scientific reputation.

What he hoped to do was map the route of one of the vanished glaciers—tracing it so thoroughly, by the scratches it had left on the rocks and by the layers of debris and rubble it had piled up, that no one could have further doubt that rivers of ice had flowed through Yosemite. All through May and June, 1871, whenever he could get away from his duties at Hutchings' sawmill, he tracked his lost glacier through the upper reaches of the park. Patterns began to take shape for him. He found a string of moraines, deposits of glacier-borne debris. He noticed that the canyons most deeply shadowed by the high peaks were the ones where glacial scratches were most abundant, as though the shadowed areas, by keeping the temperature low, had allowed the glaciers to thrive more vigorously than on the sunny slopes. He worked his way up and down the Sierra, measuring, comparing, analyzing. In July, to have more time for his research, he quit his job with Hutchings and moved his few belongings to a room at Black's Hotel, a new lodging house downstream near Leidig's. He was certain by then that he had identified the path of one great glacier 12 miles long and 5 miles wide that had crossed the Sierra from north to south. "Waking or sleeping I have no rest," he told Mrs. Carr on September 8. "In dreams I read blurred sheets of glacial writing or follow lines of cleavage or struggle with the difficulties of some extraordinary rock form."

From time to time he interrupted his explorations to descend into the relative civilization of Yosemite Valley, and often he found distinguished scientists eager to discuss his findings with him. In July, there was Clinton L. Merriam of the Smithsonian Institution; in August, John Daniel Runkle, president of the Massachusetts Institute of Technology. Such dignified Easterners as these frequently were dismayed by Muir's bizarre appearance when he came down out of the mountains, dressed in tatters, his lean face smeared with soot to protect him against snowburn, his clear blue eyes seemingly peering off into immense distances. His shaggy appearance and his look of strange intensity led many people to compare him to the fiery, impassioned prophets of the Old Testament or even to Jesus Christ; an artist named William Keith who met Muir about this time and became his close friend nicknamed him "the Prophet Jeremiah." But those who paid more attention to what Muir said than to the way he looked realized that he was on the threshold of valuable geological discoveries. Merriam and Runkle in particular were convinced of the truth of Muir's ideas and urged him to publish his findings in the scientific journals.

The thought of writing for publication distressed him. Since the beginning of his travels in the 1860's he had kept notebooks, spending hours each day filling them with descriptions of all he had seen and done. His writing, naïve and clumsy at first, had grown steadily more expert, and now he was the master of a splendid style, both lyrical and precise. But the notebooks had been written for his eyes alone. To have something printed and read by the scholars of the Eastern universities was a frightening prospect; it made him self-conscious and ashamed of his literary and scientific shortcomings. Still, it was something to consider. Writing books or magazine articles was a way of earning a living. Having left Hutchings, he was now unemployed, and though in his thirfty Scots way he had managed to lay aside savings of $500, he would have to think about making money again when that was gone. His own expenses were low, but he was sending money east to help pay for his sister Mary's college education, since the tightfisted Daniel Muir had as usual refused to contribute anything. It might be necessary, then, for him to go back to guiding tourists in 1872—unless he started earning money with his pen. "Some of my friends are badgering me to write for some of the magazines, and I am almost tempted to try it," he said in his September 8 letter to Mrs. Carr, "only I am afraid that this would distract my mind from my main work more than the distasteful and depressing labor of the mill or of guiding. What do you think about it?" Perhaps it would be wiser, he added, to wait until he had completed his glacial studies and then write a comprehensive book that would "prove that each dome and brow and wall, and every grace and spire and brother is the necessary result of the delicately balanced blows of well directed and combined glaciers against the parent rocks which contained them. . . ."

On September 24, 1871, Muir wrote a long letter to Dr. Merriam, summarizing his findings and discussing some of his most recent discoveries. When he finished it and reread it, he realized that he could combine this letter with one he had recently sent to President Runkle and produce a respectable short essay on the origin of Yosemite. Quickly he did the necessary carpentry work of revision, and on September 28 he mailed a piece called "The Death of a Glacier" off to the New York *Tribune*. To his great amazement, it was accepted, paid for, and published, under the title of "Yosemite Glaciers," in the issue of December 5, 1871. And the *Tribune* asked him for further contributions. He promptly ransacked his recent correspondence and put together two more pieces, "Yosemite in Winter" and "Yosemite in Spring," which the *Tribune* ran on January 1 and May 7, 1872. Thus he made his debut as a professional writer.

The articles were well received in the East. The first one was reprinted in the January, 1872, issue of *Silliman's Journal,* a scientific publication. Professor Samuel Kneeland of the Massachusetts Institute of Technology used it, along with some of Muir's letters to Dr. Runkle, as the basis for a paper, "On the Glaciers of the Yosemite Valley," that he delivered before the Boston Society of Natural History on February 21, 1872. Muir was flattered by the attention his views were getting, though he grumbled a bit about Kneeland, who, he said, gave him "credit for all the smaller sayings and doings and stole the broadest truth to himself."

While Muir's reputation was building in scientific

circles, he was living through exciting days in Yosemite. In October, 1871, wandering among the mountains of the Merced group, he came upon a small stream carrying mud of a kind he had not seen before. "In a calm place where the stream widened," he reported to Mrs. Carr, "I collected some of this mud and observed that it was entirely mineral in composition and fine as flour—like mud from a fine grit sandstone. Before I had time to reason I said, 'Glacier mud!—mountain meal!' "

Looking around, Muir beheld a bank of stones and dirt some 60 or 70 feet high, with a "raw, unsettled, plantless, new-born appearance." Surely this was a glacial moraine, a heap of rubble dumped here by a moving glacier! He scrambled to its top and saw what seemed to be a huge snowbank, close to 500 yards long and half a mile wide. "Embedded in its stained and furrowed surface were stones and dirt like that of which the moraine was built. Dirt-stained lines curved across the snow-bank from side to side, and when I observed that these curved lines coincided with the curved moraine, and that the stones and dirt were most abundant near the bottom of the bank, I shouted, 'A living glacier!' " He had suspected all along that small glaciers still lingered in the Sierra—and now he had found one, living proof of his theory. In the course of the next two years he would discover more than sixty others.

A month later, as winter closed in, he went off toward the northeast, past the steep-plunging Tuolumne Canyon, and for the first time entered the

Hetch Hetchy Valley, "one of Nature's rarest and most precious mountain temples." This was a valley much like Yosemite itself, a sister valley, though somehow less formidable, less monumental. In some ways it was even more beautiful than Yosemite, for tourists did not go there and its floor was unmarred by hotels, cottages, trash dumps, or trails. Descending into it by way of a path made by bears, he explored it and left convinced that it had been shaped by the same glacial forces that had formed Yosemite. In a letter to his mother of November 16, 1871, he said, "The few scientific men who have written upon this region tell us that Yosemite Valley is unlike anything else, an exceptional creation, separate in all respects from all other valleys, but such is not true. Yosemite is one of *many,* one chapter of a great mountain book written by the same pen of ice which the Lord long ago passed over every page of our great Sierra Nevadas."

In mid-December a titanic storm swept through Yosemite—a "jubilee of waters," Muir called it, three days of raging winds and pounding rains that whipped streams into wild floods. He went out into it, glorying in the elemental furies of nature unleashed. On New Year's Day he recast the notes he had taken on this event into the form of an article, "Yosemite Valley in Flood," and sent it off to Mrs. Carr for an opinion. A notable passage of the piece criticized the California State Park Commission for its desecration of Yosemite's natural beauty for the sake of "vulgar, mercenary 'improvement.' " It marked the beginning of his development into a crusader for the protection of the environment.

Nature provided another diversion for Muir at half past two in the morning on March 26, 1872. He was awakened by "a strange wild thrilling motion and rumbling" and ran from his cabin, "both glad and frightened, shouting, 'A noble earthquake!' feeling sure I was going to learn something." Perhaps Yosemite had not been formed by an earthquake, as Josiah Whitney insisted, but the valley was not immune to them. Muir, wanting to experience the event as intimately as possible, rushed about from place to place, but the shocks "were so violent and varied, and succeeded one another so closely, one had to balance in walking as if on the deck of a ship among the waves, and it seemed impossible the high cliffs should escape being shattered. In particular, I feared that the sheer-fronted Sentinel Rock, which rises to a height of three thousand feet, would be shaken down, and I took shelter back of a big pine, hoping I might be protected from outbounding boulders."

Sentinel Rock did not fall, and for a few moments all was still. "Then, suddenly, out of the strange silence and strange motion there came a tremendous roar. The Eagle Rock, a short distance up the valley, had given way, and I saw it falling in thousands of the great boulders I had been studying so long, pouring to the valley floor in a free curve luminous from friction, making a terribly sublime and beautiful spectacle—an arc of fire fifteen hundred feet span, as true in form and as steady as a rainbow, in the midst of the stupendous roaring rock-storm." Even before the wreckage had settled, Muir was climbing the huge blocks of stone. Some frightened Indians and a few whites spending the winter in the valley had gathered by now in front of the Hutchings Hotel. Muir found them pale and worried, and tried to cheer them with jokes, telling them, "Smile a little and clap your hands. Mother Earth is only trotting us on her knee to amuse us and make us good!" But there were no smiles. Failing to share Muir's delight in the great convulsion, they saddled their horses and got out of the trembling valley as fast as they could, leaving the "madman" Muir alone to savor the aftershocks that came near dawn.

8

A Rising Career

The summer of 1872 saw John Muir on his way toward becoming a public figure, an eccentric but profound prophet speaking out of the western mountains. His articles were now appearing every month or so in the New York *Tribune* and were being discussed in scientific circles throughout the East. Meanwhile, the Carrs had sent his essay on Yosemite in flood to the *Overland Monthly,* a well-known magazine of the day published in California; the piece was accepted and appeared in the April, 1872, issue. It was so popular with the readers that he was asked to do another, which appeared in July, and thereafter he became a regular contributor to the *Overland.*

Famous scientists who visited California made a point of seeking Muir out in his mountain retreat. The great British physicist John Tyndall toured the Sierra with Muir early in the summer of 1872 and a few months later sent him, as a gift, a hundred dollars' worth of delicate scientific instruments for use in his research. Then came Asa Gray of Harvard, the world's leading botanist, whom Muir had been writing to for several years, sending him specimens for Boston's botanic garden. The next visitor was another famed botanist, the aged John Torrey, Asa Gray's own teacher. Muir looked forward also to a visit from Louis Agassiz, whose pioneering work on glaciers had inspired his own studies. Agassiz reached San Francisco in August, but his health would not permit a trip to Yosemite, to Muir's deep disappointment. Muir sent Agassiz a long letter, describing his work among the glaciers of the Sierra and trying to tempt him into coming; when he read it, Agassiz exclaimed to his wife, "Here is the first man who has any adequate conception of glacial action." He promised to return in a year or two and spend an entire summer with Muir in the mountains, but death took him first.

When not entertaining these distinguished visitors, Muir continued to discover and survey the living glaciers of the Sierra Nevada. In August, 1872, he planted five wooden stakes in a glacier he had found on Mount McClure, east of the Yosemite Valley. Returning to the stakes after forty-six days, he found that the glacier had carried all five of them downstream; the stake closest to the glacier's midpoint had traveled almost four feet, a rate of about an inch a day. Thus he proved that the deposits of ice on these mountains were no mere snowbanks, but rather were living, flowing glacial rivers.

The climax of Muir's mountain adventures came

that fall when he climbed 13,300-foot Mount Ritter—"the king of the mid-Sierras," as he called it. No one yet had reached the summit of this great peak. Muir's new friend, the Scottish-born artist William Keith, was looking for some spectacular mountain scenery to paint, and so Muir took Keith and two other artists on a camping trip up the Tuolumne River. One morning, leaving them to their sketchbooks, Muir set out alone, on foot, to ascend Mount Ritter. He needed a whole day to reach the point where his climb would begin. Then, crossing a glacier, he started to work his way up a sheer granite cliff covered with ice. He was scarcely past the halfway mark when he was forced to halt, clinging to the face of the rock, unable to see any footholds ahead. "Suddenly," he wrote, "my danger broke upon me. Faith and hope failed, suffered eclipse. Cold sweat broke out. My senses filled as with smoke. I was alone, cut off from all affinity. Would I fall to the glacier below? Well, no matter. . . ." But then he felt a "strange influx of strength." His nerves ceased to quiver; his eyes, made more keen by peril, sought and found "every rift, flaw, niche, and tablet" in the cliff ahead, "as through a microscope." The danger was past. "Shortly after noon I leaped with wild freedom into the sunlight upon the highest crag of the summit. Had I been borne aloft upon wings, my deliverance could not have been more complete."

It was a godlike sensation to stand there, looking out at "the incomprehensible grandeur, variety, and abundance of the mountains rising shoulder to shoulder," seeing the pathways carved by the glaciers—"eloquent monuments of the ancient ice-rivers"—and staring down into mile-deep canyons. To the east lay the burning sands of the Mono Desert; to the west, the gray granite towers of the Sierra swept off in wild ridges toward the peaceful coastal valleys. Not until the sun was low did Muir begin his descent, scrambling down across an ice cascade where a glacier had shattered into massive blocks separated by deep blue fissures. At sunset he reached the mountain's eastern base. Warm purple light bathed the Mono country. "The peaks marshaled along the summit were in shadow, but through every notch and pass streamed vivid sunfire, soothing and irradiating their rough, black angles, while companies of small, luminous clouds hovered above them like very angels of light." In darkness he found his way back to his lakeside camp. At dawn he was up; he splashed cold water in his face, enjoyed his usual breakfast of bread and tea, and thawed himself awhile in the morning sunshine. Then he proceeded on to the Tuolumne camp where he had left the three painters, reaching them at dusk.

He made two more mountain excursions that fall to check on the positions of his glacier stakes. When he returned from the second one, late in November, William Keith urged him to go with him to Oakland. His friends there, the Carrs and Le Contes and others, were eager to see him, and several important magazine editors wanted to meet him. Grudgingly Muir consented. But he regretted it as soon as he reached civilization. He had not set foot in any city since the one day he had spent in San Francisco four and a half years earlier, and after the tranquillity of the Sierra and the lowland valleys, he found the heavily populated area around San Francisco Bay too much for him. By day his friends hustled him back and forth to art galleries, museums, libraries, and editorial offices; by night they bombarded him with strangers at noisy parties held in his honor. He met some people who would be important to him in his new career as a writer, and he formed some rewarding new friendships; but after two weeks he needed to escape. "I was so frightened out of more than half of each of my senses by the blaze and glare of everything about me," he told his brother David, and to his sister Sarah he wrote, "I was terribly dazed and confused with the dust and din and heavy sticky air of that low region." Hurriedly he boarded an eastbound train that took him as far as the town of Turlock; from there he literally ran toward the mountains, hardly resting until he was safe in Yosemite.

Now there was new ecstasy in feeling "the living electric granite" beneath his feet, in clearing his lungs of "dead city air." He embarked enthusiastically on a series of winter trips. One of these, in late December, brought him his closest brush with death. He was crossing Tenaya Canyon, something no one had yet succeeded in doing, and was working his way along a spur where glaciers had polished the rock smooth. Suddenly he slipped, falling backward, turning several somersaults, and striking his head on the granite. He lost consciousness, and when he came to, he found that he had rolled almost to the brink of the canyon; a few short, stiff bushes right at the edge had snagged him and kept him from going over. His momentary clumsiness made him feel "degraded and worthless," and he spoke harshly to his erring feet, telling them, "That is what you get by intercourse with stupid town stairs and dead pavements!" To punish himself for having lost his footing, he made himself sleep that night on a bare boulder instead of a pillow of boughs, and the next day guided "my humbled body over the most nerve-trying places I could find."

That winter Muir was treated to a rare and wonderful sight: snow banners blowing across the Sierra. This happens when a strong north wind whips and swirls snow crystals against rocks and trees until they are broken to fragments and become a sort of fine icy dust. Then the wind scoops this snow dust from exposed slopes and hurls it into the air, forming great ribbonlike banners that stream from the peaks, a mile or more in length and more than a thousand feet wide. In all of Muir's years in the mountains he saw this only once, on a morning when he was awakened "by the rocking of my cabin and the beating of pine-burs on the roof." Avalanches were tumbling down the side canyons, and a fierce storm tore at the trees. The wind was so fierce that the cascade of Yosemite Falls was blown sideways, revealing the cone of ice that forms in winter at its foot. Wishing to inspect this cone while he had the chance, Muir left his cabin, but as he approached the falls, "the peaks of the Merced group came into sight over the shoulder of the South Dome, each waving a resplendent banner against the blue sky, as regular in form, and as firm in texture, as if woven of fine silk." Forgetting about the ice cone, Muir at once began to clamber up an avalanche-choked canyon for a better view of this phenomenon, and after four hours of climbing through the roaring storm he stood atop a ridge 8,000 feet high. "And there in bold relief, like a clear painting, appeared a most imposing scene," he reported. "Innumerable peaks, black and sharp, rose grandly into the dark blue sky, their bases set in solid white, their sides streaked and splashed with snow, like ocean rocks with foam; and from every summit, all free and unconfused, was streaming a beautiful silky silvery banner, from half a mile to a mile in length, slender at the point of attachment, then widening gradually as it extended from the peak. . . ."

Such spectacular scenes as this went into the articles that Muir now was turning out at a steady pace. Writing was terribly hard work for him; he labored to achieve a vivid, luminous style, searching patiently for the exact words, struggling against his tendency to overuse such adjectives as "glorious" and "noble" and "stupendous." But though he wrote and rewrote and rewrote again, muttering and sweating over every line, his notebooks contained the raw material for so many exciting essays that he could not help being highly productive. In April, 1873, he informed Mrs. Carr that he had ideas for more than two dozen pieces—on forests, lakes, avalanches, earthquakes, birds, bears, and his own Sierra adventures—and expected to be mailing them to her at a rate of about one a month. He kept to this busy schedule. The April *Overland* ran his account of his Tenaya Canyon mishap, followed a couple of issues later by a piece on Hetch Hetchy Valley and then one on Grand Tuolumne Canyon. The editor of the magazine now referred to him as "our leading contributor" and begged Muir for more articles.

The summer of 1873 saw Muir making his most ambitious journeys yet. First came five weeks of explorations in the mountains east of Yosemite; then, at the beginning of September, he made his first thrust into the Kings River region, 100 miles south of the territory he now knew so well. His companions on this trip were Dr. Albert Kellogg, a botanist, and William Simms, an artist. Their first stop was the Wawona lodge of the Yosemite pioneer Galen Clark, and Muir, looking for an experienced climbing partner, persuaded Clark to go with them. Muir's journal of the trek opens with a somber comment on the devastation worked by sheep in the meadows near Wawona: "The grass is eaten close and trodden until it resembles a corral. . . . Nine tenths of the whole surface of the Sierra has been swept by the scourge. It demands legislative interference." Muir could not understand why sheep were still allowed to graze freely in Yosemite Park.

They pushed southward at a slow pace. On the ninth day Muir, growing impatient, left the party for a four-day excursion through the mountains of the San Joaquin Basin. He discovered fifteen glaciers and saw, wherever he looked, valleys of the Yosemite type—"a mass of ice sculpture." When he rejoined the others, he spoke with his usual fervor about those snowy peaks and suggested further high-country rambles. Clark, who was not a young man, groaned at the suggestion and abruptly decided that he really ought to be back at Yosemite performing his duties as guardian of the park. "Clark is going to leave us," Muir wrote to Mrs. Carr on September 27. "Told me five minutes ago. Am a little nervous about it, but will of course push on alone."

Now all the responsibilities of leadership were upon him, for neither Kellogg nor Simms had had much experience as a mountaineer. All went well, however. They crossed the divide between the South Fork of the San Joaquin River and the North Fork of the Kings, then traversed the terrain between the North and Middle forks of the Kings, camping in glacial valleys and immense forests. Giant sequoias grew here, and in early October they entered the first grove of these colossal trees. This was well-traveled country; from settlers in the grove Muir learned that as many as fifty tourists had been there in the last six weeks. The main attraction was a tree nicknamed General Grant, 267 feet tall and 40 feet thick at ground level. Muir measured the circumference of this giant among giants and found the tree's girth to be 106 feet. "The 'General Grant' is burned near the ground on the east side," he observed, "and bulges in huge gnarly waves and crags on the north and west. Its bole above the base thirty or forty feet is smooth and round." He was saddened to see how visitors had mutilated the grand old tree by "hacking off chips and engraving their names in all styles." Seven years later Muir would begin his ultimately successful fight to preserve these sequoia groves within the confines of a national park.

Beyond the big trees lay the mighty Kings River Canyon, "with all that is most sublime in the mountain scenery of America." Huge mountains soared on all sides. Leaving Kellogg and Simms camped, Muir took off for solitary ascents of 14,000-foot Mount Tyndall and several nearby peaks, almost as mighty, that did not then have names. Returning to the camp, he found that his two companions were gone, having left neither horse nor provisions for him. Muir tracked them all day across dry meadows and through the "savage and desolate scenery" of a pass 12,000 feet high, catching up with them at sunset. "When asked why they had left me, they said they feared I would not return," he wrote. "Strange that in the mountains people from cities should so surely lose their heads."

Muir's next goal was Mount Whitney, the tallest peak in the United States. (Sixteen mountains in Alaska surpass it, but Alaska was not then a state.) Clarence King of the California Geological Survey had discovered it in 1871 and had named it in honor of the state geologist, Josiah Whitney, Muir's old nemesis. King had supposedly climbed Mount Whitney at the time of its discovery. Once again leaving his companions below, Muir, on October 15, 1873, gained the summit of the peak identified on his chart as Mount Whitney and immediately realized that King, two years earlier, must have become confused during his ascent by the multitude of mountains clustered here. For Muir could see another mountain, five or six miles to the north, that was obviously several hundred feet taller than the one he had just conquered. King had somehow failed to climb the real Mount Whitney.

Muir hastened that same day to the other mountain. At sunset he reached a small lake at the base of its highest crag. His food was gone, and he saw no wood to make a fire, so he decided to spend the night climbing. About eleven o'clock he reached the crest; the temperature was 22 below zero, and he had no coat, no blanket. Above him still loomed one last spire, several hundred feet high. He made several attempts to go on, but the intense cold and thinness of the atmosphere robbed him of strength, and he felt a dangerous drowsiness overtake him. To keep from falling asleep he broke into a wild dance, leaping, waving his arms about, clapping his hands; then he sank down exhausted, and as sleep crept up on him again, he began to dance once more. In this desperate way he passed the night. At dawn, feeble and starving, he made a new try at scaling that final peak, but he grew dizzy and weak. "I felt," he said, "as if Someone caught me by the shoulders and turned me around forcibly, saying 'Go back' in an audible voice." For once admitting defeat, he went down the mountainside.

He spent two days in camp, resting, eating, and studying his charts, and on October 19 started again to climb what he believed to be the true Mount Whitney. This time he went up the eastern side, and at eight in the morning on October 21 he attained the summit. Messages found in a tin can at the top told Muir he had not been the first to get there. A climber named Carl Rabe had succeeded on September 6, and Clarence King had followed him thirteen days later. King's note told how "clouds and storms" had caused his mistake of 1871. But no one had ascended the mountain from its eastern face before Muir.

Geographers eventually agreed on new names for these lofty peaks. The one King had climbed in 1871, 14,028 feet high, became Mount Langley. The 14,494-foot peak conquered three times in 1873 was identified as the real Mount Whitney. And the neighboring crest, 14,015 feet high, where John Muir was forced to halt and dance all night to keep alive, now bears the name of Mount Muir.

After the descent from Mount Whitney, Muir, Kellogg, and Simms started northward up the eastern base of the Sierra through the edge of the Mono Desert. They parted from him at Lake Mono, but Muir continued on alone for another hundred miles or so, to the shores of Lake Tahoe, before heading back to Yosemite. He was in his cabin again by the middle of November, having covered a thousand miles of wilderness, discovered a great many new glaciers and glacial valleys, and tested himself against some of the continent's greatest mountains.

Now, despite his bad experience of the year before, he was bound for Oakland again. "I suppose I must go into society this winter," he wrote to his sister Sarah on November 14, 1873. "I would rather go back in some undiscoverable corner beneath the rafters of an old garret with my notes and books and listen to the winter rapping and blowing on the roof." But he could not allow himself the luxury of spending the coming winter as a hermit in the mountains. The *Overland Monthly* had agreed to publish a lengthy series of articles, under the general title "Studies in the Sierra," that would sum up all he had learned in his five years among the glaciers. He needed reference books that were not available to him at Yosemite; he might need, also, to consult with his editors. Perhaps, too, he felt he had been cutting himself off too willingly from the rest of mankind. "You must be social, John," Mrs. Carr had told him, "you must make friends . . . lest your highest pleasures, taken selfishly, become impure." Though he loved the mountain solitudes, he realized that he loved the company of human beings as well, and in December he set out for Oakland. He hoped to live with the Carrs while writing his articles, but when he arrived he found them in mourning over the death of their eldest son; he took lodging instead at the home of another friend, J. B. McChesney, Oakland's superintendent of schools.

He took care this time to avoid the whirl of parties and outings that had exhausted him in 1872. Though he did not hide from society, he remained housebound a good deal of the time, diligently working on the seven essays of his "Studies in the Sierra" and some less ambitious magazine pieces. As always, writing was a torment for him. Words seemed inadequate—mere "mist rags"—to describe the things he had seen. He was hard put to select a few telling details out of such a horde of wonders: "As soon as one begins to describe a flower or a tree or a storm or an Indian or a chipmunk," he complained, "up jumps the whole heavens and earth and God Himself in one inseparable glory!" In a letter to his father he told of the fatigue his work was causing him, but Daniel had no consolation to offer. Replying in March, 1874, he told his son, "You cannot warm the heart of the saint of God with your cold icy-topped mountains. O, my dear son, come away from them to the spirit of God and His holy word. . . . And the best and soonest way of getting quit of the writing and publishing your book is to burn it, and then it will do no more harm either to you or others." But of course, Muir persevered at his desk, and the first in his Sierra series appeared in the May, 1874, *Overland.*

It was not only a time for work, but for the renewing of old friendships and the cultivation of new ones. Now that he was a recognized authority on glacial matters, the scientific community of the Bay area welcomed him among them. He spent many evenings with Professor Le Conte, with the Carrs, with the painter William Keith, and with the learned John Swett, the state superintendent of schools. Mrs. Carr also saw to it that Muir had the occasion to meet the Strentzel family, owners of a large fruit ranch in the Alhambra Valley near Martinez, California. John Strentzel was a Polish-born physician who had fled the political uprisings of Europe in 1840 to settle in the United States; after living in Kentucky and Texas, he had come to California in 1849 with his wife and baby daughter as medical adviser to a group of pioneers. He had purchased land east of San Francisco in Contra Costa County and, using advanced scientific agricultural methods, had become a prosperous fruit grower. His wife, an intelligent, well-read woman, had been following Muir's articles in the *Overland.* In the spring of 1874 she noted in her diary, "How I should love to become acquainted with a person who writes as he does. What is wealth compared to a mind like his! And yet I shall probably never see him."

Then there was the Strentzels' daughter, Louie Wanda. She was twenty-seven years old that year, a quiet, dark-haired girl, fond of flowers and music, who, after her graduation from college, had given up a promising career as a concert pianist to remain on her father's ranch. She shared the responsibilities of running it with her father and had shown herself to be a shrewd and capable businesswoman. Though many men had sought to marry this highly eligible heiress, Louie had refused them all, waiting for the right man. Mrs. Carr thought she had found that man for her. In 1872 she had written to Louie, "I want you to know my John Muir. I wish I could give him to some noble young woman 'for keeps' and so take him out of the wilderness into the society of his peers."

Muir, vaguely aware of the plans Mrs. Carr was hatching, took care to keep his distance whenever he and the Strentzels were in Oakland at the same time. But in the summer of 1874 a meeting finally came about. He was thirty-six years old, a confirmed bachelor who had known few moments of romance, and his first conversation with Louie Strentzel must have been a lame, awkward thing. But as he was taking his leave, her parents warmly invited him to visit them at their ranch. Muir said he would, but set no specific time.

By September, 1874, he was finished with his seven Sierra articles and a number of other pieces. After ten months in Oakland, he was finished with city life, too, for a while. An overpowering impulse to escape possessed him, and without even bothering to settle accounts with his publishers, he caught a Sierra-bound train. Once again he got off at Turlock, and, he wrote to Mrs. Carr, "next morning faced the Sierra and set out through the sand afoot. The freedom I felt was exhilarating, and the burning heat and thirst and faintness could not make it less. Before I had walked ten miles I was wearied and footsore, but it was real earnest work and I liked it.

Any kind of simple natural destruction is preferable to the numb, dumb, apathetic deaths of a town."

And from Black's Hotel in Yosemite he exulted, "Here again are pine trees, and the wind, and living rock and water!" But he felt a curious detachment from his familiar haunts. "No one of the rocks seems to call me now, nor any of the distant mountains. Surely this Merced and Tuolumne chapter of my life is done. . . . I feel that I am a stranger here. . . . I will go out in a day or so."

He allowed himself a lingering farewell to Yosemite, though, revisiting this canyon and that for four weeks. Not until October 15 was he on his way, northward bound toward California's Mount Shasta by way of Lake Tahoe. Glaciers lay deep on the flanks of that great peak, and the surrounding countryside, not yet marred by lumbermen and mining companies, was wild and beautiful. Muir got his first glimpse of Shasta one morning as he tramped a dusty road in the hot Sacramento Valley and the mountain suddenly came into view: "I was fifty miles away and afoot, alone, and weary. Yet all my blood turned to wine, and I have not been weary since." He wrote that on November 1, at Shasta's foot. Later that day he began his climb. A local guide, Jerome Fay, accompanied him as far as the high timberline, but Muir went on to the utmost summit by himself, starting at half past one in the morning. By 10 A.M. he was on top, and spent two hours tracing the routes of living glaciers. Then, with a storm coming on, he descended to his camp at the 9,000-foot level. "It stormed wildly and beautifully," he wrote, but he was snug beneath thick woolen blankets in a hollow between some trees and a lava block. He had a week's supply of food, which he knew he could stretch to two or even three weeks if he had to. Notebook in hand, he emerged from his shelter to study snowflakes with a magnifying glass, to observe crows and squirrels and wild sheep, to enjoy the howl of the gales. On the third day he wrote, "Wild wind and snow. Drifts changing the outlines of mountains—pulsing outlines. Three inches of snow on my blankets. Sifted into my hair. Glorious storm!" The next day, to Muir's annoyance, Jerome Fay appeared, riding one horse and leading another. He had come to "rescue" Muir, who, though he had not felt himself endangered, now had to break camp and descend to the lodge at the foot of the mountain.

Late in December, 1874, he left Shasta to visit a friend of his boyhood days, Emily Pelton of Prairie du Chien, Wisconsin, who was living in a small town about 50 miles north of Sacramento. Here, too, Muir indulged his love of storms. The day after his arrival he was roaming a forest of huge trees along one of the tributaries of the Yuba River; the weather was dry, clear, and sunny, but the wind was strong, and rapidly grew stronger, until Muir found himself in "one of the most bracing wind-storms conceivable." Trees 200 feet tall "waved like supple goldenrods chanting and bowing low as if in worship. . . . Nature was holding high festival, and every fiber of the most rigid giants thrilled with glad excitement." Another man might have fled, but Muir drifted happily on from ridge to ridge, listening to the song of the wild winds ripping through the treetops, even attempting to distinguish "the varying tones of individual trees—spruce, and fir, and pine, and leafless oak—and even the infinitely gentle rustle of the withered grasses at my feet." About midday he gained the summit of the highest ridge in the neighborhood, and, seeking to go higher still, had the notion of climbing one of those flailing trees. Near him was a clump of young Douglas spruce, about 100 feet in height, "their lithe, brushy tops . . . rocking and swirling in wild ecstasy." He picked the tallest and sturdiest in the group, and up he went, scaling the tree with ease. It "flapped and swished in the passionate torrent, bending and swirling backward and forward, round and round, tracing indescribable combinations of vertical and horizontal curves," while Muir, muscles firmly braced, hung on "like a bobolink on a reed." From that lofty, dizzying perch he calmly surveyed the hills, the trees waving like fields of rippling grain, the shimmering light reflected from the needles of pine and spruce. He stayed there for hours, closing his eyes to concentrate on "the keen metallic click of leaf on leaf" and "the profound bass of the naked branches and boles booming like waterfalls," dismounting only when the storm had abated. Who but John Muir would have given himself over to such an event? A few days later, when he went out into a snowstorm and returned late at night, drenched and half frozen, his hosts offered their sympathy, but

Muir, face blazing with a prophet's zeal, replied, "Don't pity me. Pity yourselves. You stay here at home, dry and defrauded of all the glory I have seen. Your souls starve in the midst of abundance!"

9

Among the Sequoias

Early in 1875 Muir returned to Oakland for another bout of writing. "I am bound to my studies, and the laws of my own life," he said in a letter to his sister Sarah at the end of February. "At times I feel as if driven with whips, and ridden upon." Yet his arduous researches had given his life a center. He had no home, no family, no regular occupation, but his travels and his literary work provided him with a sense of accomplishment. "The world, as well as the mountains, is good to me," he told Sarah, "and my studies flow on in a wider and wider current by the incoming of many a noble tributary."

There was an increasingly conservationist tone to his thinking and writing. The wilderness that he loved was being destroyed by farmers, miners, and loggers, and he felt a need to speak out while there still was something left to save. So urgent did the problem seem that he even conquered his perpetual shyness and agreed to deliver a lecture on the destruction of the environment before the Literary

Institute of Sacramento in January. Though nervous and frightened, he handled his first public-speaking assignment with great success and later undertook many more such engagements. He put forth his conservationist views in print for the first time in an article for the Sacramento *Record-Union* on February 5, 1875, in which he argued for state control over forest usage in place of the existing easygoing approach. If nothing were done about wasteful and greedy logging, large-scale grazing of sheep in the Sierra, and the practice of setting fire to the forests to clear them for livestock, there soon would be no forests in existence. "Whether our loose-limbed Government is really able or willing to do anything . . . remains to be seen," he wrote. But he called for new forestry legislation.

In April Muir ascended Mount Shasta again, leading a party of scientists who wanted to make barometric observations. While at the summit, he and the guide Jerome Fay were caught by an unexpected storm; unable to return to their timberline camp, they took refuge for the night at a volcanic hot springs near the top, a place where sulfurous fumes belched forth and ponds of boiling mud burbled and spat. Huddling in his shirt sleeves with icicles in his beard, alternately pelted with driving snow and scalding mud, Muir endured fourteen miserable hours, his only comfort coming from the contemplation of the "tranquil radiance [of] the mysterious star-clouds of the milky way." At daybreak he and Fay stumbled down to their camp, lame with frostbite. Weeks later Muir was still hobbling, and he would feel the effects of that freezing night for the rest of his life.

He was back in the Sierra Nevada in June, with a commission to write a series of articles for the San Francisco *Bulletin*. His first trip that summer took him through the Yosemite region with his friends William Keith, J. B. McChesney, and John Swett. Then, on July 9, he went south toward the Kings River area, accompanied by a San Franciscan named George Bayley and a university student, Charles Washburn. Entering one grove of giant sequoias near the North Fork of the Kings, Muir heard the sound of axes and soon came upon a group of men busily cutting up a huge tree, 25 feet in diameter at the base. He was appalled to learn that they had chopped it down so that a 16-foot-long section could be shipped to Philadelphia for exhibition at the 1876 Centennial Exposition. A count of the growth rings visible on the stump showed that the felled giant had lived more than 2,100 years before perishing for such a trifling reason. "Many a poor, defrauded town dweller will pay his dollar and peep, and gain some dead arithmetical notion of the bigness of our Big Trees," Muir said in one of his *Bulletin* articles, "but a true and living knowledge of these tree gods is not to be had at so cheap a rate. As well try to send a section of the storms on which they feed."

There was more cause for dismay ahead, in the great canyon on the South Fork of the Kings. Three sheep owners had nailed an ominous sign to a pine tree: *"We the undersigned claim this valley for the purpose of raising stock, etc."* Muir warned his *Bulletin* readers to "visit the valley at once, while it remains in primeval order." Describing the devastation that had come to the similar glacial valleys of the Merced and Tuolumne after they had been turned into pastures for sheep, hogs, and cattle, he predicted that "all the destructible beauty" of this southern canyon "is doomed to perish like that of its neighbor. . . ."

After climbing Mount Whitney a second time, Muir returned to Yosemite on July 31, but in a few weeks he was on his way back to the Kings River region, this time alone except for an agile little brown mule. It was his usual custom to do his mountaineering on foot, but this promised to be a long trip—an extended survey of the groves of sequoias south of Yosemite—and the mule would be handy for carrying provisions and blankets.

After visiting the Mariposa grove, Muir struck out toward the southeast, into an unexplored valley. Here he found no giant sequoias—Big Trees, he called them—until he ascended a towering granite dome in early September and looked into the valley of the Fresno River. "Away toward the southwest," he wrote, "on the verge of the glowing horizon, I discovered the majestic domelike crowns of Big Trees towering high over all, singly and in close grove congregations." Heading into this grove, he settled beside a brook, made a cup of tea, and went forth to inspect these giants. The first thing he found was a landslide site, seven or eight years old, where the ground had given way on one side of a stream to a depth of about 50 feet. Many trees had been uprooted, but Muir was cheered to see sequoia seedlings and saplings growing on the upturned soil along the landslide's front face: "These young trees were already eight or ten feet high, and were shooting up vigorously, as if sure of eternal life. . . . Farther down the ravine I counted 536 promising young sequoia on a bed of rough bouldery soil not exceeding two acres in extent."

Giant sequoias fascinated John Muir—as indeed they had fascinated everyone who had ever seen them. Their first discoverers, of course, had been the Indians. The first white man to behold them was probably Zenas Leonard of Pennsylvania, a member of an expedition that crossed the Sierra Nevada from east to west in 1833. But they did not come to public attention until 1852, when a hunter named A. T. Dowd found one while pursuing a wounded bear deep into a Sierra forest in Calaveras County, California. When Dowd returned to town with news that he had come upon a huge reddish tree as wide as a house and so tall he could not see its top, his friends jeered; but he talked them into coming back with him into the forest, and they looked with awe on the amazing tree—one of more than 150 clustered in a 50-acre grove. Great excitement followed, as curiosity seekers rushed to look upon the titans.

Botanists, studying the trees, eventually realized that they were related to another tribe of forest giants, the redwood trees of the California coast. The coast redwoods—which had been given the scientific name of *Sequoia sempervirens,* "ever-living sequoia," in honor of the nineteenth-century Cherokee chief Sequoyah—had straight trunks, dark red-brown in color, that rose to heights of more than 300 feet, making them the tallest trees on earth. These inland trees of the Sierra Nevada were not quite so tall, averaging about 250 feet. But whereas the coastal trees were comparatively slender, 12 to 15 feet thick at ground level, the trees of the Sierra had immense bases, with thicknesses of 25 or 30 feet common and some specimens approaching 40 feet. Thus they were far more massive than the taller coastal trees and weighed as much as 6,000 tons apiece. Scientists dubbed them *Sequoia gigantea*; they received an assortment of popular names, such as "Sierra redwood," "giant Sequoia," and Muir's favorite, "Big Tree," but are most often called giant sequoias today.

While in the grove at the landslide site Muir discovered a hermit—"an old, weary-eyed, unspeculative, gray-haired man"—living in a log cabin. He was John A. Nelder, a pioneer who had failed to strike it rich in the gold rush of 1849 and who had been living alone among the forest giants to wait out his last days. Muir tells how Nelder "tenderly stroked the little snow-bent sapling sequoias, hoping they might yet grow straight to the sky and rule the grove. One of the greatest of his trees stands a little way back of his cabin, and he proudly led me to it, bidding me admire its colossal proportions and measure it, to see if in all the forest there could be another so grand. It proved to be only 26 feet in diameter, and he seemed distressed to learn that the Mariposa Grizzly Giant was larger. I tried to comfort him by observing that his was the taller, finer formed, and perhaps the more favorably situated." (The Grizzly Giant is the fifth largest known giant sequoia, in terms of bulk. Though only 209 feet high, its diameter is 28 feet, its circumference is 96.5 feet, and it contains 30,300 cubic feet of wood.)

The grove where Nelder dwelled covered about four square miles, making it one of the biggest groupings of giant sequoias ever discovered. "One of the most interesting features of this grove," said Muir, "is the apparent ease and strength and comfortable independence in which the trees occupy their place in the general forest. Seedlings, saplings, young and middle-aged trees, are grouped promisingly around the old patriarchs, betraying no sign of approach to extinction. On the contrary, all seem to be saying, 'Everything is to our mind, and we mean to live forever.' " But would the promise of those young sequoias be fulfilled? "Sad to tell," Muir added, "a lumber company was building a large mill and flume nearby, assuring widespread destruction." So it came to pass. Logging operations began in the Nelder Grove a few years later, and today only 200 acres of giant sequoias—less than a third of a square mile—survive there, part of Sierra National Forest.

Leaving the hermit, Muir and his mule moved on,

"day after day, from grove to grove, canyon to canyon," traveling "a long wavering way; terribly rough in some places for Brownie, but cheery for me, for sequoias were seldom out of sight." In one Kings River grove Muir found a "majestic stump," 140 feet high and 35 feet 8 inches thick just above the swell of the roots. This dead sequoia, he reported, "was burned nearly half through at the base, and I spent a day in chopping off the charred surface, and cutting into the heart, and counting the wood-rings with the aid of a lens. I made out a little over four thousand without difficulty or doubt, but I was unable to get a complete count, owing to confusion in the rings where wounds had been healed over." Muir's 4,000-year-old sequoia stump has since disappeared; if he made no error in the count, this was the oldest sequoia ever found, though many in the 3,500-year range are known.

A sawmill was busy in this Kings River grove, "forming a sore, sad center of destruction." Only the smaller and more accessible trees were being cut when Muir was there, but he knew the turn of the titans would soon come. "The logs, from three to ten or twelve feet in diameter, were dragged or rolled with long strings of oxen into a chute and sent flying down the steep mountainside to the mill flat, where the largest of them were blasted into manageable dimensions for the saws. . . . By this blasting and careless felling on uneven ground, half or three-fourths of the timber was wasted."

In the valley of the Kaweah River, beyond the

North Fork of the Kings, Muir came one day at sundown to a sequoia grove so imposing that he named it the Giant Forest. "It extends," he wrote, "a magnificent growth of giants, grouped in pure temple groves, ranged in colonnades along the sides of meadows, or scattered among the other trees, from the granite headlands overlooking the hot foothills and plains of the San Joaquin back to within a few miles of the old glacier fountains, at an elevation of five thousand to eight thousand four hundred feet above the sea."

He walked through the groves until sundown; then he made his simple supper and lay on his back, "looking up to the stars through pillared arches. . . ." By moonlight, the trees "seemed still more marvelously massive and tall than by day, heaving their colossal heads into the depths of the sky among the stars, some of which seemed to be sparkling on their branches like flowers." Muir was up at dawn, and all through the long, mellow autumn day he sauntered among the sequoias, watching the changing colors from hour to hour. Suddenly the spell was broken: A man on horseback appeared at the far end of the grove. He was a rancher named Hale Tharp, who had been grazing his livestock in the Kaweah Valley for many years. He had become friendly with the local Indians, and in 1858 they had led him to this place of immense trees. Tharp went back there in 1860 and made a summer home for himself, 58 feet long and 8 feet high, in a single fallen sequoia that had been hollowed out by fire. Adding a door, window, chimney, and entrance foyer, Tharp had occupied his tree house every summer while his herds were in the valley. For seventeen years—until this meeting with Muir in 1875—he had been the only white man to know of the Giant Forest. Now he was so surprised at seeing a stranger that he could not speak, and it was Muir who hailed him, saying he was glad to meet a fellow mountaineer in such a lonely place.

"What are you doing?" Tharp asked. "How did you get here?"

Muir explained that he had come "across the canyons from Yosemite, and was only looking at the trees."

"Oh, then, I know," Tharp replied. "You must be John Muir."

Tharp was herding a band of horses in the forest meadows. Since Muir was nearly out of food, he asked the rancher if he could spare a little flour. "Oh, yes, of course, you can have anything I've got," Tharp said, telling Muir how to reach his cabin, a few miles away. Then he galloped off to round up some strayed horses. Muir saddled Brownie and arrived at the cabin by midafternoon—"a spacious log house of one log, carbon-lined, centuries old, yet sweet and fresh, weatherproof, earthquake-proof, likely to outlast the most durable stone castle." Soon Tharp came in, and the two mountaineers ate and talked a long while about the great trees.

There were hundreds of giants here, including the biggest Big Tree of all, the one that later would be called the General Sherman Tree, 272 feet high, 37 feet thick at the base, containing enough wood to build forty five-room houses. There was also the 291-footer that would be the McKinley Tree, the 250-foot President Tree, and the vast Lincoln Tree, 259 feet high and 31 feet in diameter at ground level.

In another forest between the Middle and East forks of the Kaweah Muir found a fire in progress, "and as fire is the master scourge and controller of the distribution of trees, I stopped to watch it and learn what I could of its works and ways with the giants." Tethering Brownie in a safe place, he went into the fire area and made a camp for himself in a sturdy hollow trunk. Then he roamed about, night after night, watching the spectacular show: "Big bonfires blazing in perfect storms of energy where heavy branches mixed with small ones lay smashed together in hundred-cord piles, big red arches between spreading root-swells and trees growing close together, huge fire-mantled trunks on the hill-slopes glowing like bars of hot iron, violet-colored fire running up the tall trees, tracing the furrows of the bark in quick quivering rills, and lighting magnificent torches on dry shattered tops, and ever and anon, with a tremendous roar and burst of light, young trees clad in low-descending feathery branches vanishing in one flame two or three hundred feet high." To Muir the forest fire was no cause for lamentation; it was part of nature's own cycle and therefore nothing to regret. The big trees had survived many such fires in their thousands of years of life, and most of them would survive this one.

On he went southward into the valley of the Tule River, where he found yet another grand forest of sequoias. But large flocks of sheep had swept the valley bare of grass, and there was nothing for Brownie to eat. Muir shared his own last remnant of bread with the hungry, weary mule and a day later led him down to the foothills, where he obtained some barley from a farmer. Then Muir went on, until he realized he had come to the end of the 250-mile-long sequoia belt. By November he was back in San Francisco to spend the winter writing.

It had been a journey of wonders and marvels, but at journey's end Muir's exhilaration was mingled with forebodings and fears. How long would those phenomenal trees endure? Already he could hear the voice of the sawmill, "moaning like a bad ghost," in the groves. His zeal for conservation had never been stronger. "Wildness is a necessity," he wrote. "Mountain parks and reservations are useful not only as fountains of timber . . . but as fountains of life."

Now came a busy time of writing and lecturing. "My life these days is like the life of a glacier, one eternal grind, and the top of my head suffers a weariness at times that you know nothing about," he told his sister Sarah in the spring of 1876. His articles were appearing steadily in the *Bulletin,* the *Overland,* and other California newspapers and magazines. He had also begun to contribute to *Harper's Magazine,* one of the most widely read and influential periodicals in the nation. Though he wrote mainly about his own experiences, conservationist themes were ever more prominent in his work.

His most important literary project in 1876 was his piece on the sequoia belt of the Sierra Nevada. It was published in the highly respected *Proceedings of the American Association for the Advancement of Science* under the title "On the Post-Glacial History of *Sequoia Gigantea.* By John Muir, of San Francisco, Cal." This masterly article clarified much that had been previously unknown about these trees: Muir showed that they were found only in the high inland country, but that they were plentiful there and in no danger of extinction from natural causes. If left alone, the sequoias would continue to reproduce and sustain themselves. Unfortunately, he said, "*man* is in the woods, and waste and pure destruction are already making rapid headway." Five sawmills were in operation; one had "cut over two million feet of Big Tree lumber last season. . . . It appears, therefore, that notwithstanding our forest king might live on gloriously in nature's keeping, it is rapidly vanishing before the fire and steel of man; and unless protective measures be speedily invented and applied, in a few decades at the farthest, all that will be left of *Sequoia gigantea* will be a few hacked and scarred monuments."

While continuing to make frequent short visits to the Sierra, he was starting to broaden the range of his explorations. In May, 1877, he went to Utah, clambering over the peaks and canyons of the Wasatch Range and swimming in the Great Salt

Lake. "It was the finest water baptism I ever experienced," he declared. "Salted, braced, I ran bounding along the beach with blood tingling as if I had discovered a new glacier." Then it was on to Lake Tahoe and Yosemite, and into southern California for "a fine shaggy little five days' excursion back in the heart of the San Gabriel Mountains." Up the coast, next, to inspect the redwoods of the Santa Cruz Mountains, then to lecture at the San Jose Normal School. In August two great botanists, Asa Gray and Sir Joseph Hooker, arrived in San Francisco and asked Muir to guide them to Mount Shasta, where the three scientists prowled about enthusiastically in search of rare blossoms. Then he took a voyage with some friends down the Sacramento River in a skiff and concluded this remarkably busy summer with a trek into the almost inaccessible Middle Fork country of the Kings River. With a boat of his own making he floated 250 miles westward again down the Merced and San Joaquin rivers, coming to rest one late November day in the town of Martinez. A two-mile hike into the Alhambra Valley brought him to the Strentzel ranch, where, after a three-year lapse, he finally took advantage of Dr. Strentzel's invitation. He spent most of his time talking about scientific matters with the doctor, but it seems he found the opportunity to speak to Louie Strentzel as well.

December saw him back in San Francisco once more, a guest at the home of his friend John Swett. His wanderings had left him looking disheveled and wild, as usual. Mrs. Swett wrote, "After his long trip he stood there . . . in a faded greenish-hued coat rather out at the elbows and wrist, his beautiful hair hanging down almost to his shoulders, and I wondered how his appearance had impressed Louie Strentzel. It worried me . . . that he had made his acquaintance with this girl in such a plight."

In the winter of 1877-78 he produced more articles for *Harper's* and contributed his first essay to an even more distinguished magazine, *Scribner's Monthly,* perhaps the finest periodical then being published. The editors of *Scribner's* were so pleased that they asked him to send them all his future work.

Frequently in the spring of 1878 Muir visited the Alhambra Valley to see Louie Strentzel and take her on long walks into the hills. He was falling in love, beyond any doubt: a strange and unsettling thing to happen to a forty-year-old man. If he married Louie Strentzel, he knew, he would have to surrender much of the freedom that enabled him to tramp the mountain country for months on end, but possibly he had allowed himself too much of that freedom and had let another part of life slide by, unsampled. To his sister Sarah he wrote, "Little did I think when I used to be, and am now, fonder of home and still domestic life than any of the boys, that I only should be a bachelor, and doomed to roam always outside the family circle."

But for the time being he made no commitments. The wilderness still called him. In June, the U.S. Coast and Geodetic Survey invited him to take part in an expedition to Nevada, and he accepted—though his friends, especially the Strentzels, tried to persuade him not to go, for Indian disturbances had made that region unsafe for some years. The explorers started from Sacramento, crossing the Sierra to Lake Tahoe and pushing into the desert. "All goes well in camp," he wrote to the Strentzels on July 11. "All the Indians we meet are harmless as sagebushes, though perhaps about as bitter at heart." Muir enclosed some wild prunes, praising their flavor and suggesting that Dr. Strentzel try cultivating them. He found them too sour and sent some of his juiciest grapes to show Muir what good fruit was *really* like.

Muir searched the Nevada desert for traces of the presence of ancient glaciers, hoping to extend the evidence that a giant ice sheet once had covered most of the continent. For some weeks he saw no signs of glaciation, but then, near the town of Belmont, he discovered moraines, glacial carvings, "and even feeble specimens of glacier meadows and glacier lakes." However, the effects of time "have not simply obscured the glacial scriptures here," he told the Strentzels, "but nearly buried and obliterated them, so that only the skilled observer would detect a single word, and he would probably be called a glaciated monomaniac." He concluded, "Now it is clear that this fiery inland region was icy prior to the lake period."

Late in August two of the government surveyors decided to climb Lone Mountain, 40 miles from the nearest water supply. Muir, against his better judgment, let himself be talked into going with him. "On Lone Mountain we were *thirsty,*" he reported to the Strentzels. "How we thought of the cool singing streams of the Sierra while our blood fevered and boiled and throbbed!" When their water gave out, they experienced terrible hardships, Muir suffering less than the others, "though I suffered as never before." He was the only one strong enough to descend the mountain and look for and fetch the horses they had left below. "Then I had to find my two companions. One I found death-like, lying in the hot sand, scarcely conscious and unable to speak above a frightful whisper. I managed, however, to get him on his horse. The other I found in a kind of delirious stupor, voiceless, in the sagebrush. It was a fearfully exciting search, and I forgot my own exhaustion in it, though I never for a moment lost my will and wits, or doubted our ability to endure and escape. We reached water at daybreak of the second day—two days and nights in this fire without water!" The rest of the journey was less arduous. They crossed through the White Pine mining district, which had played out and was a region of ghost towns, and entered Utah. Then, as was now his custom, he returned to San Francisco at year's end. On January 28, 1879, he wrote to the Strentzels, "The vast soul-stirring work of flitting is at length done and well done. Myself, wooden clock, and notebooks are once more planted for the winter out here on the outermost ragged edge of this howling metropolis of dwelling boxes." A heavy schedule of writing awaited him.

He was planning, now, a jaunt through the forests of Washington and British Columbia for the summer of 1879. In June, though, he went to Yosemite as one of the guest speakers at a nationwide convention of Sunday-school teachers being held there. Muir spoke on "The Geological Records of the Yosemite Valley Glaciers," and, according to the San Francisco *Chronicle,* he "fairly electrified his audience, and over a hundred followed him up the Eagle Point Trail. . . . This was fun for him for he leaped over the crags like a goat. . . ." One of the other lectures had Alaska as its subject, and Muir, listening to it, was so fascinated that he decided to go there.

First, however, he paid a call at the Strentzel ranch. He had resolved to make Louie his wife. He spoke with her most of an evening, and about midnight she went to her mother's room. "All's well, Mother. All's well, and I'm so happy," she whispered. But the engagement was to be kept secret for a while. Not even Mrs. Carr was told. Writing to her a few weeks later, Muir merely said, "I'm going home—going to my summer in the snow and ice and forests of the north coast. Will sail tomorrow at noon on the *Dakota* for Victoria and Olympia. Will then push inland and alongland. May visit Alaska."

10

To the North

The Puget Sound region was Muir's first stop on his northward voyage. Hiring a boat, he sailed the length of the sound three times, from Oregon deep into British Columbia, exploring as many of the side routes as he could and looking up in awe and delight at the great fir-clad, glacier-crowned Olympic Mountains bordering the water. After a few weeks of this he went on to Alaska aboard the steamship *California,* docking at the Indian town of Fort Wrangell on Alaska's lower coast.

There he met a youthful and lively missionary, S. Hall Young. Though Muir's boyhood experiences had left him wary of those whose profession was religion, he struck up an immediate friendship with Young, who invited him to accompany him on his rounds among the Alaskan tribes. Soon they were on their way up the coast together in a river steamer. At one point Young took time off from his holy toil to go mountain climbing with Muir, but he was a novice at such activities and, slipping on a sheer precipice, nearly fell to his death. Muir caught him by the belt and trousers as he grabbed some rocks and virtually carried the shaken and injured Young down from the mountain.

In October, Muir and Young arranged to go on a canoe voyage to the north, guided by an old Indian named Toyatte. As the plans for the trip were being completed, Muir received a letter from Louie Strentzel. "So far, so far away," she wrote, "and still another month of wandering in that wild North-land. . . . I shiver with every thought of the dark cruel winter drifting down, down—and never a beam of sunshine on all that wide land of mists . . . what a blessed Thanksgiving if only you come home." But he could not let his fiancée's longing for him—or his for her—interfere with his Arctic adventure. "Surely you would not have me away from this work, dawdling in a weak-willed way on your lounge, dozing and drying like a castaway ship on the beach," he replied, adding a brusque postscript: "Leave for the North in a few minutes. Indians waiting. Farewell."

Up they journeyed through the maze of islands along the Alaskan coast. Four Indians were with them, three to paddle, and old Toyatte, a master of the winds and tides, standing in the canoe's stern and steering. Their goal was an inland bay of glaciers and icebergs that the natives called Sitadaka, which no white explorer had ever seen. The Indians were reluctant to go near the place, believing it haunted.

Muir tells us how "they talked in tones that accorded well with the wind and waters and growling torrents about us, telling sad old stories of crushed canoes, drowned Indians, and hunters frozen in snow-storms." But Toyatte obediently obtained directions from Indians of the upper coast and brought Muir and Young to their goal.

In mid-October they arrived at the edge of the bay and made camp near the westernmost glacier. Because it was Sunday, Young would go no farther that day. Muir was bothered by the missionary's observance of the Sabbath, which seemed "weak and craven out here in the wilds where God himself works on Sunday. We should keep ourselves in right relations to Nature—come and go at her bidding." Leaving Young in camp, he set out alone to see the bay. Climbing a ridge 1,500 feet high, Muir "gained some noble views of five glaciers that pour their crystal floods directly into the salt water. . . . The clouds hung low . . . but every now and then I gained glimpses of a wide sea of ice in which the mountains rise like islands in the white expanse." Thus he became the first white man to see this legendary place, now Glacier Bay National Monument.

After a day spent trekking through rain and mud and sludgy snow, wading and jumping across icy streams, and wallowing in shoulder-deep snowdrifts, he returned to camp, drenched and chilled, to find a sort of mutiny in progress. The Indian guides, who had stayed in camp with Young because the weather was so bad, had given way to their fears of the demons of the bay and wanted to turn back. Today's rainstorm seemed a bad omen to them; they were sure it meant the spirits were angry and would overturn the canoe. "They seemed to be losing heart with every howl of the wind," Muir wrote, "and, fearing that they might fail me now that I was in the midst of so grand a congregation of glaciers, I made haste to reassure them, telling them that for ten years I had wandered alone among mountains and storms, and good luck always followed me; that with me, therefore, they need fear nothing." Muir's straightforward self-confidence encouraged the Indians, and Toyatte declared that his heart was strong again, saying that he would not greatly care if the demons sank the canoe, "because on the way to the other world he would have good companions."

For the next five days they explored "dim, dreary, mysterious" Glacier Bay, prowling among the glaciers under a constant downpour of rain and snow. Muir was in his proper element. The glaciers of the Sierra were trifles compared to what he found here, and he reveled in the frosty beauty of the bay. On the second day he climbed a mountain until he was above the rain: "Sunshine," he wrote, "streamed through the luminous fringes of the clouds and fell on the green waters of the fiord, the glittering bergs, the crystal bluffs of the vast glacier, the intensely white, far-spreading fields of ice, and the ineffably chaste and spiritual heights of the Fairweather Range, which were now hidden, now partly revealed, the whole making a picture of icy wildness unspeakably pure and sublime." Not even nightfall could halt him, for he was too excited to sleep more than a few hours: "I stole quietly out of the camp, and climbed the mountain that stands between the two glaciers. The ground was frozen, making the climbing difficult in the steepest places; but the views over the icy bay, sparkling beneath the stars, were enchanting. It seemed then a sad thing that any part of so precious a night had been lost in sleep. The starlight was so full that I distinctly saw not only the berg-filled bay, but most of the lower portions of the glaciers, lying pale and spirit-like amid the mountains. The nearest glacier in particular was so distinct that it seemed to be glowing with light that came from within itself. . . . Everything was more or less luminous, and I seemed to be poised in a vast hollow between two skies of almost equal brightness."

The fifth day brought the grandest sight of all: an immense glacier—now called the Muir Glacier—along the eastern shore of one of the fjords connected to the bay. "I was strongly tempted to go and explore it at all hazards," Muir said. "But winter had come, and the freezing of the fiords was an insurmountable obstacle." Reluctantly he left Glacier Bay on October 31, with the great glacier unexamined.

Now they paddled southward, calling at various Indian towns along the coast so that Young could do some preaching and converting. Though the weather was steadily worsening, Muir insisted on a number of side trips up the innumerable coastal inlets, and several times they were nearly capsized in the wintry mists by sandbars or icebergs. Muir, who had caught sight of another major glacier in an unexplored bay, recklessly forced them to go on and on. At last Toyatte, who had a far more realistic attitude toward the dangers of the region in this season than Muir, told him that he had no right to risk all their lives merely to gratify his curiosity. Muir saw the truth of this and gave up the chase, not without vowing to himself to return next year and find that "lost glacier."

At the end of November he was back at Fort Wrangell. It had been a highly successful expedition, for he had seen living glaciers in action and had verified many of the conclusions of his "Studies in the Sierra." But he found unhappy letters from Louie Strentzel waiting for him. She was troubled by the hardships she imagined he was enduring and worried, too, by the length of his separation from her—which, she knew, would be followed inevitably by other long separations during their married life. "I dare not call to lead you from the way that you feel best," she told him, but there was no doubt that the conflict between his work and their love was causing her to suffer.

Still, he prolonged his absence from her by some months more. By January, 1880, he was only as far south as Portland, Oregon, where he was asked to give a series of lectures. The fee that was offered was tempting to a man about to get married, and he accepted. He did not reach California until

February; by the middle of that month he was at the Strentzel ranch to help in the wedding preparations. Announcements went forth to his astonished friends, setting a date of April 14.

Nature supplied an appropriately tempestuous setting for John Muir's wedding. A tremendous rainstorm that day left the town of Martinez and the surrounding countryside awash in floods. But everything went off on schedule, and somewhat to his own amazement, Muir found himself a married man, one week before his forty-second birthday. He and Louie settled into the Strentzel home, the elder Strentzels taking up residence elsewhere on the ranch. Muir rented a section of the orchards and vineyards from his father-in-law and, the day after the wedding, began to apply his usual vigor and enthusiasm to the study of raising fruit. For the next three months he labored in the fields as he had as a young man—no longer his father's miserable slave, though, but rather the master of his own estate. He had an occupation at last: fruit rancher.

By July the crops were ripening, and the summer lull settled over the ranch, with harvest season three months away. By agreement with his wife, this would be John Muir's time each year for a journey in the wilderness—a period of escape from domestic captivity and a rancher's obligations. On July 30 he sailed north aboard the *Victoria*.

By August 8 he was at Fort Wrangell. The missionary S. Hall Young had come down to the wharf to pick up the monthly mail delivery the ship was carrying, and to his immense surprise, he saw John Muir standing on deck. Muir ran down the gangplank and greeted Young with a sudden question: "When can you be ready?" As Young stood there, gaping and speechless, Muir cried out, "Man, have you forgotten? Don't you know we lost a glacier last fall? Do you think I could sleep soundly in my bed this winter with that hanging on my conscience? . . . Get your canoe and crew and let us be off!"

Young, when he recovered from his shock, quickly agreed to organize a second canoe trip for Muir. Old Toyatte was dead, killed in a brawl during the winter while trying to act as a peacemaker, but Young found another expert Indian boatsman, Lot Tyeen, who was willing to take Muir on a voyage of a month or more at a cost of $60 per month. They set out in mid-August. The party included, besides Muir, Young, and Lot Tyeen, two other Indians: Lot Tyeen's son-in-law, Hunter Joe, and a half-breed named Smart Billy. At the very last moment the crowded canoe acquired another passenger. Down to the wharf came Young's little black dog, Stickeen—named for the local Indian tribe, the Stikines or Stickeens. He jumped into the boat, Muir wrote, and "immediately made himself at home by curling up in a hollow among the baggage. I like dogs, but this one seemed so small and worthless that I objected to his going." Young assured him that Stickeen would be no trouble at all, that he was "a perfect wonder of a dog, could endure cold and hunger like a bear, swim like a seal, and was wondrous wise and cunning, etc. . . ."

Stickeen was allowed to go along. "Nobody could hope to unravel the lines of his ancestry," Muir said. "In all the wonderfully mixed and varied dog-tribe I never saw any creature very much like him." He had the sly, soft, gliding movements of a fox; his hair was long and silky, his ears were thin and sensitive, his eyes sharp and cunning; his only really distinguished feature was "his fine tail, which was about as airy and shady as a squirrel's, and was carried curling forward almost to his nose." As the canoe moved northward through Wrangell Narrows and the intricate island-dotted channels beyond, Stickeen kept to himself, "in sluggish ease, motionless, and apparently as unobserving as if in deep sleep." But whenever they neared shore for a landing, he was always the first one over the side, swimming vigorously to the beach and disappearing in the woods in search of squirrels and birds. He could never be found when it was time to leave, but as soon as the canoe pushed off, he would reappear, swimming out toward the boat. "We tried to cure him of this trick," said Muir, "by compelling him to swim a long way, as if we had a mind to abandon him; but this did no good: the longer the swim the better he seemed to like it."

In a few days they reached Holkham Bay, where Muir had seen his "lost glacier" of 1879. The bay proved to have two arms. Entering the eastern one first, Muir discovered a glacier three-quarters of a mile wide and 800 or 900 feet deep, which he named

Young Glacier. A second glacier lay just beyond. Then they crossed into the bay's other arm, entering through a rock-walled channel that Muir deemed a new Yosemite Valley in the making. The canoe traveled more than 20 miles up the western arm until at last a glacier came in view. "There is your lost friend," the Indians said to Muir, and as icebergs broke loose from it, toppling into the water with a sound like thunder, they added, "He says, *Sagh-a-ya,* How do you do!"

When he had charted his glaciers, Muir went onward through Stephens Passage. Camping on Douglas Island, he noticed a geological formation that he believed probably contained gold. The next day he met two prospectors, Joe Juneau and Joe Harris, and told them about it. They went to inspect, and indeed struck gold there—touching off a gold rush that led to the founding of the town of Juneau.

Wherever Muir wandered on the Alaskan shore, the dog Stickeen tagged behind him, forsaking his own master. He "always insisted on going with me, however wild the weather," Muir said. "Once he followed me over a glacier the surface of which was so crusty and rough that it cut his feet until every step was marked with blood; but he trotted on with Indian fortitude until I noticed his red track, and, taking pity on him, made him a set of moccasins out of a handkerchief." Yet Muir was unable "to make out what Stickeen was really good for." He never obeyed an order and showed none of the usual doggish signs of affection: "No matter what advances you might make, scarce a glance or a tail-wag would you get for your pains. But though he was apparently as cold as a glacier and about as impervious to fun, I tried hard to make his acquaintance, guessing there must be something worthwhile hidden beneath so much courage, endurance, and wild-weathery adventure." Stickeen seemed to have no need of love; he asked only to be let alone and allowed to go on his own way.

On August 29 they camped at the mouth of an inlet now known as Taylor Bay. A large glacier, "rounded like a snout," lay nearby. The Indians of the region reported that the glacier was moving at a rate of about a mile a year; Muir could see the trees that had recently been toppled along the shore by its latest advance. Eager to be out and on it, he arose before dawn, during a tremendous rainstorm, and, making a breakfast of "bread and rain," slipped away from the camp. All the others still lay sleeping—all but Stickeen, who came bounding out of a tent and rushed after him. Muir tried to persuade the dog to go back, but Stickeen would not listen. "This wild day has nothing for you," Muir told him. "There's no game abroad, nothing but weather. Go back to camp and keep warm, get a good breakfast with your master, and be sensible for once. I can't carry you all day or feed you, and this storm will kill you." But, Muir wrote, "I saw that he was not to be shaken off; as well might the earth try to shake off the moon." He gave Stickeen a corner of the crust of bread he had in his pocket, and off they went together on what

Muir called "the most memorable of all my wild days."

All morning they skirted the edge of the glacier, picking their way through the forests of uprooted trees. Three miles north of the glacier's front Muir climbed to its top, cutting steps for himself and Stickeen with an ice ax. "As far as the eye could reach, the level, or nearly level, glacier stretched away indefinitely beneath the gray sky, a seemingly boundless prairie of ice. The rain continued, and grew colder, which I did not mind, but a dim snowy look in the drooping clouds made me hesitate about venturing far from land." Nevertheless, the ice was firm, and he decided to cross the immense glacier from side to side. The trek took hours. The going was easy at first, but toward the far side the glacier was split by tremendous crevasses, some of them 20 or 30 feet wide and 1,000 feet deep, "beautiful and awful." Muir circled around the bigger ones, and jumped over those that were only 4 or 6 feet wide. "In working a way through them I was severely cautious," he said, "but Stickeen came on as unhesitatingly as the flying clouds. The widest crevasse that I could jump he would leap without as much as halting to take a look at it. . . . The little adventurer was only about two years old, yet nothing seemed novel to him, nothing daunted him. He showed neither caution nor curiosity, wonder nor fear, but bravely trotted on as if glaciers were playgrounds." Muir was aghast as Stickeen blithely sailed across crevasses 6 or 8 feet in width.

The glacier proved to be 7 miles from one side to the other. Reaching the far edge, Muir turned northward again, going as far as he could toward the glacier's source before the onset of dusk suggested to him that he ought to head back to camp. As night came on, the rain turned to snow, and Muir "began to feel anxious about finding a way in the blurring storm." To make things even worse, the homeward route was broken by an infinity of crevasses of appalling width. The glacier seemed to be shifting and heaving, and these great cracks in its surface were increasing in number and size. Muir considered the possibility that he would come to a crevasse too wide to jump and too long to go around, and would have to spend the night on the glacier, desperately dancing to stave off the cold.

Ahead of him now loomed a crevasse a dozen feet wide at its narrowest point. "The width of this jump was the utmost I dared attempt," said Muir, "while the danger of slipping on the farther side was so great that I was loath to try it." For a long time he stared at the crevasse, estimating distances carefully, calculating his chances of making it. Perhaps it would be wiser to admit defeat and climb down the glacier's side into the woods. But that certainly meant a night of cold and hunger, and the ice beyond the crevasse looked more promising, giving him the hope of getting back to camp that evening if he jumped. "At length, because of the dangers already behind me, I determined to venture against those that might be ahead," he wrote, and he "jumped and landed well," though with little to spare. "Stickeen followed, making nothing of it, and we ran eagerly forward, hoping we were leaving all our troubles behind. But within the distance of a few hundred yards we were stopped by the widest crevasse yet encountered."

This gash in the glacier was 40 to 50 feet across. There was no hope of jumping that; Muir sought instead to find an end he could go around. Following the crevasse one way, he discovered that it did not end at all, but simply curved back to run into the one he had just jumped. When he went the other way, he found it was the same. He was on an island of ice, and at no point was the crevasse in front of him less than 40 feet in width.

There was one possibility for getting across. When this crevasse had been formed, the ice had failed to split in one point, leaving a sliver-thick bridge of ice spanning it from side to side. This bridge was about 70 feet long, crossing the crevasse diagonally; at its ends it was some 8 feet below the surface of the glacier, but it drooped in the middle to a depth of 30 feet. To reach the bridge at all, Muir would have to descend a vertical wall of ice for those 8 feet; then he had to cross the bridge itself, knowing that a slip or a sudden strong gust would send him toppling into an abyss. "Of the many perils encountered in my years of wandering on mountains and glaciers none seemed so plain and stern and merciless as this. And it was presented when we were wet to the skin and hungry, the sky dark with quick driving snow, and the night near. But we were forced to face it. It was a tremendous necessity."

A little to one side of the bridge he cut a deep hollow on the brink of the crevasse with his short-handled ax. Kneeling in this, he reached down and cut a step 16 or 18 inches below. He put his feet in it and, steadying himself against the wind, hacked another step below it, and another, and another, with "life and death . . . in every stroke." Lowering himself from step to step, he reached the bridge of ice and sat straddling it. "Crossing was then comparatively easy by chipping off the sharp edge [of the bridge] with short, careful strokes, and hitching forward an inch or two at a time, keeping my balance with my knees pressed against the sides. The tremendous abyss on either hand I studiously ignored. To me the edge of that blue sliver was then all the world." Eventually—it seemed to take years—he reached the far side. Now he had to cut a second ladder for himself in the shining vertical wall of the crevasse—"chipping, climbing, holding on with feet and fingers in mere notches. At such times one's whole body is eye, and common skill and fortitude are replaced by power beyond our call or knowledge. Never before had I been so long under deadly strain. How I got up that cliff I never could tell. The thing seemed to have been done by somebody else."

But Stickeen was still on the other side. While Muir had first been cutting his ladder down the crevasse, the dog had muttered and whined at him, as if to say, "Surely, you are not going into that awful place." Now Muir was across, and Stickeen, showing fear for the first time, would not follow him. Crying, peering into the gulf before him, he ran away, seeking some other crossing, finding none, returning finally to the brink, "moaning and wailing as if in the bitterness of death. Could this be the silent, philosophic Stickeen? I shouted encouragement, telling him the bridge was not so bad as it looked, that I had left it flat and safe for his feet, and he could walk it easily. But he was afraid to try. Strange so small an animal should be capable of such big, wise fears." Muir called again and again, but Stickeen only howled in terror. "I was troubled at the thought of having to leave him out all night, and of the danger of not finding him in the morning. It seemed impossible to get him to venture. To compel him to try through fear of being abandoned, I started off as if leaving him to his fate, and disappeared back of a hummock, but this did no good; he only lay down and moaned in utter hopeless misery." So, going back to the brink, Muir shouted across to the dog in a severe tone of voice that he could wait no longer and that, if Stickeen would not come, he could promise no more than to return the next day to look for him. He urged the dog one final time to cross, and this time, "with the courage of despair," Stickeen crouched down, huddling close to the ice, and took the first step. He bunched all four feet into one step, his head down, and eased himself into the notch below, until he was on the bridge. He crossed it easily, holding himself steady against the buffeting wind. But now the hardest task was at hand, for dogs are poor climbers, and he had to ascend the ice ladder on the far side. Muir watched him "looking keenly into the series of notched steps and finger-holds I had made, as if counting them, and fixing the position of each one in his mind. Then suddenly up he came in a springy rush, hooking his paws into the steps and notches so quickly that I could not see how it was done, and whizzed past my head, safe at last!"

Now came the celebration: Stickeen darted and scampered about, rolling over and over, running in giddy loops and circles, dashing wildly at Muir and almost knocking him down, "all the time screeching and screaming and shouting as if saying, 'Saved! saved! saved!' " After a time he grew calm, and they moved on again across ice gashed by thousands of crevasses—"but they were common ones. The joy of deliverance burned in us like fire, and we ran without fatigue." By ten o'clock they were back in camp. Young and the Indians had almost given up hope. A big fire was blazing, and a supper of porpoise meat and wild goat was ready, but Muir and Stickeen were too tired to eat and lay down at once to sleep.

After that, Stickeen often would come to him and rest his head on his knee with a look of devotion "as if I were his god. And often as he caught my eye he seemed to be trying to say, 'Wasn't that an awful time we had together on the glacier?' "

But Stickeen was Young's dog, and he stayed behind in Alaska when Muir departed for home a few weeks later. He had to be carried away, crying and struggling, as Muir's steamer pulled away, and Muir never saw him again. The story of his adventure, though, traveled on. Muir told the tale over and over, until it became so famous that wherever he went people wanted to hear about Stickeen. For seventeen years he worked at writing the story down, forever redoing his account for the sake of capturing Stickeen more fully in words and of showing how, from their shared experience, he had drawn a renewed knowledge of the kinship of our "horizontal brothers" and "the vertical mammal," man. Not until 1897 was he finally satisfied to let the story be published. The little book won great popularity and still has many readers, for it is one of the finest dog stories ever told.

11

Ranching Days

The second Alaskan trip, brief though it had been, yielded Muir a rich harvest of data. He had gone "to read the ice record," and he certainly had. He had seen glaciers in action—sometimes rather too close for comfort—and he had gathered a great deal of information about the rate and intensity of their flow and about the way they bore down on the land to carve valleys of the Yosemite type. With that behind him, he expected to stay at home awhile, for he had a wife and a ranch to occupy him. And in March, 1881, came a baby daughter, who was named Annie Wanda.

But domestic life seemed not to agree with him. He developed nervous indigestion and was plagued by a perpetual cough. As spring neared, he was haggard and gaunt, weighing little more than 100 pounds. Louie, knowing what the best cure for such troubles would be, urged him to take a trip in his beloved mountains, but he insisted on remaining at her side.

Toward the end of April Muir went to Oakland to attend a banquet in honor of the captain and officers of the government ship *Thomas Corwin,* which was about to sail for the northern parts of Alaska and Siberia in search of a polar exploration ship, the *Jeannette,* lost since 1879. Captain Hooper of the *Corwin* invited Muir to go along. He refused, claiming family responsibilities, but when Louie heard the story the next day, she told him he should have accepted. To visit the remote Arctic, she said, would be a rare opportunity for his work, and his health demanded some kind of escape into adventure now. It was not hard for him to yield to her argument, and he was on board the *Corwin* when it sailed on May 4.

On the way north the ship hit rough seas, and Muir was seasick for the first time in his life. But he adapted quickly. Soon he was thoroughly enjoying the crashing waves and screeching winds, his cough disappeared, and he acquired "a savage, all-engulfing appetite." The bracing cold was the right medicine for him. In his letters to Louie he boasted of how much he was eating: half a salmon trout, mounds of potatoes, double helpings of soup, four or five slices of bread at a meal.

The *Corwin* followed the Alaskan coast and turned eastward through the Aleutian Islands, coming to the northeastern edge of Siberia by late June. Muir went ashore there and took a long walk over the bleak Arctic tundra, studying the spongy carpet of mosses and grasses that covered the forever-frozen soil, and seeking out ptarmigans, plovers, snipes, and other northern birds. The natives at a trading post revealed that the missing *Jeannette* had last been seen in September, 1879, half crushed, frozen into a mass of huge blocks of ice and drifting helplessly toward the north and west. Was there any hope that her thirty-three men still survived, after two years? Perhaps they had managed to get ashore with their provisions and still were waiting for rescue somewhere. The *Corwin* crawled on, doubling back and forth through the icy Bering Sea, searching for the wrecked vessel and her crew.

Whenever his ship put ashore for food or news, Muir went exploring. "The vast, mysterious ice-field of the North stretches away beneath a dark, stormy sky for thousands of miles," he wrote Louie on July 2. "I landed on East Cape yesterday and found unmistakable evidence of the passage over it of a rigid ice-sheet from the North. . . ." A few days later he had an eerie experience on St. Lawrence Island, the largest in the Bering Sea. A few years before, 1,500 Eskimos had lived there, but famine in the severe winter of 1878-79 had killed two-thirds of them, and now seven of the ten Eskimo villages were completely empty. Muir went into these villages of the dead in company with E. W. Nelson of the Smithsonian Institution, who was collecting Eskimo artifacts for the National Museum. "We found twelve desolate huts close to the beach," Muir wrote, "with about two hundred skeletons in them or strewn about on the rocks and rubbish heaps within a few yards of the doors. The scene was indescribably ghastly. . . . Gulls, plovers, and ducks were swimming and flying about in happy life, the pure salt sea was dashing white against the shore, the blooming tundra swept back to the snow-clad volcanoes, and the wide azure sky bent kindly over all—nature intensely fresh and sweet, the village lying in the foulest and most glaring death." Muir was appalled, but Nelson moved briskly among "the shrunken bodies, with rotting furs on them," and the "white, bleaching skeletons, picked bare by the crows." Muir reported to Louie how this zealous collector enthusiastically gathered about a hundred skulls as specimens, "throwing them in heaps like a boy gathering pumpkins."

Elsewhere along the Arctic coast Muir encountered another scene of death: three sportsmen out in a boat to shoot walruses. "A puff of smoke now and then, a dull report, and a huge animal rears and falls—another, and another, as they lie on the ice without showing any alarm, waiting to be killed, like cattle lying in a barnyard!" Muir had every sympathy for the Eskimos who went out with spears to hunt for their food, but this kind of "sport" seemed mere butchery to him. The walruses were being slain not for their meat but only for their tusks, as trophies for some hunter's den. This infuriated Muir, and he was infuriated again when some "fun-, fur-, and fame-seekers" aboard the *Corwin* casually shot three polar bears without leaving the comfort of the deck. "It was prolonged, bloody agony, as clumsily and heartlessly inflicted as it could well be," he said. He despised hunting for sport. Nothing more clearly revealed man's dark nature than his treatment of "his brother beasts," Muir wrote. "From the shepherd with his lambs to the red-handed hunter, it is the same; no recognition of rights—only murder in one form or another."

There was no trace of the *Jeannette,* though the *Corwin* searched for her even in the icebound region known as Wrangell Land, so difficult to approach that no human being had ever landed there. Muir was in the party that went ashore and claimed the territory for the United States, and he collected botanical specimens which have never been duplicated. The ice pack was closing in, though, and escaping only with difficulty, the *Corwin* soon moved on to safer waters. Further Arctic exploration proved impossible on account of damage to the ship's icebreaker and rudder; by early September, Muir was on his way south. (That same month the survivors of the *Jeannette,* after months of wandering among the islands of the New Siberia group, reached open water and set out by boat for the Siberian shore. But all except one perished in the attempt.)

Muir reached home in late September. The infant he had left behind in May was now an active, squalling baby; the summer's crop was nearly ready for the harvest. He had a score of things to do at once: serve as husband and father, oversee the doings of the ranch, prepare reports for the government on Arctic botany and glaciation, ship specimens of northern plants to Asa Gray at Harvard, write magazine articles, and even rebuild the ranch house, adding two open brick fireplaces and some new windows. In addition he acted as consultant to Senator John F. Miller of California, who was drawing up two conservationist bills to be introduced in Congress. One would have extended the boundaries of Yosemite Park to protect valuable timber and water resources; the other would have created a new national park in the southern Sierra, taking in the great canyons and sequoia groves of the Kings River region. But it was too soon for such legislation. Most members of Congress were interested in exploiting, rather than in protecting, the natural resources of the West. Both bills died in committee without reaching the floor of Congress.

With their failure, Muir dropped out of public life for almost ten years. His father-in-law's health was weakening, and management of the entire Strentzel ranch fell more and more to him, for little Annie Wanda kept Louie busy. No aspect of the work was too petty for him; he insisted on doing some of the hardest and heaviest jobs with his own hands. Pouring all his tremendous energy into the ranch, he greatly expanded it, planting grapevines and fruit trees where grain and hay had been grown and clearing new land for further planting. The pruning and cultivating of the trees and vines were under his direct supervision. He looked after the grafting of plants for a higher yield of fruit and pushed the ranch's output to a record peak. Then he saw to the marketing of the crop, calling on his Scottish heritage of shrewdness in setting prices and arranging terms. He constantly opened new markets, becoming the first California fruit grower to ship grapes to Hawaii. He proved as able a businessman as he was a mountaineer, for year after year he succeeded in banking a profit of $10,000—the equivalent of $50,000 or more in modern purchasing power. The shaggy-bearded prophet of the glaciers was becoming a rich man.

But all this "money-grubbing," as he called it, had a higher purpose than the mere piling away of bank deposits. He planned to work only "until I had more money than I thought I would ever need for my family or for all expenses of travel and study, however far or however long continued." Then he would sell or lease the farm and, his loved ones forever provided for, return to his wilderness world. Meanwhile, he managed to get away into the mountains some summers, between planting time and harvest time, and no matter how hard he toiled at home, he still found opportunities to wander the nearby hills and canyons. Sometimes he took young Wanda, as he now called his daughter, with him to learn the names of flowers and birds.

The ranch gradually absorbed all his vigor, however. He no longer had time to write. Robert Underwood Johnson, Muir's editor at *Scribner's Monthly,* asked him, "Have you abandoned literature altogether? . . . Has the ink in your fountain entirely dried up?" Well-known scientists urged him to resume his glacial research. He grew restless and stale in the lowlands but refused to leave the ranch, claiming that he was needed there all year round. In the summer of 1884, worried about her husband's health, Louie pretended that *she* needed a vacation and insisted that he take her to Yosemite, Wanda remaining with the Strentzels. She had never seen the valley that meant so much to him, and now he guided her about it with pleasure, chuckling when she mistook trout for catfish or thought that every rustling in the bushes was a bear. But her worries did not lift. "I am anxious about John," she wrote her mother. "The journey was hard for him, and he looks thin and pale and tired. He must not leave the mountains until he is well and strong again."

Too soon, though, Muir felt he had to get back to the ranch. He could not trust others to run it, though he knew the work was sapping his vitality. "Time partially reconciles us to anything," he wrote about this time. "I gradually became content—doggedly contented, as wild animals in cages."

He was starting now to think of seeing his parents and brothers and sisters once again. He had corresponded steadily with most of his relatives over the years and had often sent money when they were in need, though he was barely less needy himself. But he had seen none of them since going to the Gulf of Mexico in 1867. News of the death of his brother-in-law David Galloway in September, 1884, was a grim reminder that he might not have many more chances to see some of the others. Late in December, 1884, he wrote to his brother David, saying that he hoped to return to Wisconsin for a visit some time in the coming year. "I could not come now," he said, "without leaving the ranch to go to wreck, a score of workmen without a head, and no head to be found, though I have looked long for a foreman. . . . Can't you send me some good steady fellow to learn this fruit business and take some of the personal supervision off my shoulders?"

Spring came, and summer, and there seemed no way he could get away from the ranch. Then a letter from his youngest sister, Joanna, the only member of the family born in the United States, reached him. Old Daniel Muir, now past eighty, had been living with Joanna in Kansas City for some time. In 1873, leaving his wife and children in Wisconsin, Daniel had gone to Canada as a Disciples of Christ missionary and had preached there until the cold weather and problems stemming from a broken hip had left him in feeble health. Then he had moved to Arkansas to stay with Joanna and had moved on with her family to Kansas City. Most of the other Muirs were still in Wisconsin. Now Joanna wrote to John to say that the old man had not been feeling well. A month or two later Muir experienced one of his strange flashes of intuition: turning suddenly to Louie, he said, "I am going East, because somehow I feel this morning that if I don't go now I won't see father again."

He made the trip alone, in a typically roundabout manner, going first to Mount Shasta, then to

Yellowstone National Park, where he went on a 150-mile camping trip, fell ill, and was thrown from a horse. On August 30 he arrived without warning at his brother David's store in Portage, Wisconsin. He found David gray and bent and old-looking; his sister Annie, who had tuberculosis, was thin and worn; his widowed sister Sarah seemed lost in grief. Only his mother seemed strong and serene, though in fact her health also was frail. Muir soon had them in a cheerier mood, for they all brightened greatly as their famous, long-vanished Johnnie told them tales of his adventures in the mountains and his life as a prosperous rancher. When the people of the neighborhood learned that John Muir was in town, they came crowding around by the hundreds for a glimpse of this former local boy, once considered so eccentric, who had achieved so many great things in California.

Muir tried to persuade his relatives to go with him to Kansas City, telling them it was their last chance to see Daniel Muir alive. But they had heard from Joanna that he was in reasonably good health for a man of his age and declined to make the trip. He argued with them until David and Annie agreed to accompany him; their mother felt she could not stand so long a journey, and Sarah remained behind to look after her.

The three Muirs stopped in Lincoln, Nebraska, where brother Dan, now a physician, was living. "I said, 'Dan, come on to Kansas City and see father.' 'Why?' he asked. 'Because if you don't see him now, you will never see him again. I think father will leave us in a few days.' 'What makes you think so?' said he. 'I have not heard anything in particular.' I said, 'Well, I just kind of feel it. I have no reason.' " Dan protested that he had patients to look after, but John insisted that he could leave them for a little while, saying, "You will not probably have to be away more than four or five days, or a week, until after the funeral." Dan replied, "You seem to talk as though you knew everything about it." But he yielded to John's strange insistence. Muir also summoned his sister Mary, who lived in Kearney, Nebraska, and his sister Maggie, of Crete, Nebraska.

On September 24 the Muirs gathered at Joanna's home. Indeed Daniel Muir was ill; he had been failing for about a month, his health having started to decline seriously just about the time John had received his mysterious telepathic message. Now the old man, exhausted and delirious, barely recognized his children. John, who had felt so much wrath over Daniel's harshness, his pettiness, his all-devouring piety, who had shaped his own life as a response to his father's grim-faced tyranny, now knew only love for him. "Father is very feeble and helpless," he wrote to Louie from Daniel's bedside. "He does not know me, and I am very sorry. He looks at me and takes my hand and says, 'Is this my dear John?' and then sinks away on the pillow, exhausted, without being able to understand the answer. . . . When I would repeat that I was his son John that went to California long ago and came back to see him, he would start and raise his head a little and gaze fixedly at me and say, 'Oh, yes, my dear wanderer,' and then lose all memory again. . . ."

From Joanna, Muir learned that in recent weeks Daniel had often spoken regretfully of the cruel things he had said and done to his "poor wandering son John" and his other children and expressed the hope he would be forgiven for his mistakes, warning Joanna "to govern her children by love alone." On the night of October 6 death came for him while John was with him. Seven of his eight children attended the funeral, all but Sarah, and Muir was glad of that, "for in all our devious ways and wanderings," he told Louie, "we have loved one another." He was home a few weeks later. The season of death gave way to new life: On January 23, 1886, the Muirs' second daughter was born. They named her Helen.

The infant's health was poor, and for the first year and a half of her life Muir scarcely dared leave the ranch, lest she become ill while he was away. It was a time of constant worry and uncertainty, which had its effects on his own strength. He was troubled, too, by the continuing destruction of the forests, while the federal government and the states stood idly by. His friends in San Francisco were urging him to take up his pen again and lead the fight for preservation of the wilderness.

In 1887 he did begin to write again, but it was a project of no great consequence. A publishing company asked him to edit and contribute to an elaborately illustrated two-volume set of nature studies entitled *Picturesque California,* to be sold in sections to subscribers. He saw it as a chance to slip in some arguments in favor of expanding the national park system, and he did; but mainly it was a dreary job of grinding hackwork. He quickly came to hate the assignment, and he was coming to hate the ranch, too, despite all the money it had poured into his pockets. He felt more like its prisoner than like its owner, and yearned for the old mountain days. "I am all nerve-shaken and lean as a crow—loaded with care, work, and worry," he wrote to his brother David in the summer of 1887.

He needed to escape. The following year Louie quietly arranged two opportunities for him. At her suggestion, the botanist Charles Parry asked Muir to go with him to Lake Tahoe to identify certain species of shrubs found there. Thus provided with a good scientific excuse to get away from the ranch, he accepted gladly. When he returned, in late June, his old friend William Keith, the artist, observed that it might be useful in the writing and editing of *Picturesque California* for him to take a trip up the Pacific Coast as far as Puget Sound. On the pretext of doing research for his book, Muir again seized the chance to head for the wilderness.

On the way north, he and Keith spent two days at Mount Shasta. Muir was horrified by the destruction of the forests on the great mountain's slopes: "The axe and saw are heard here more often . . . and the glory is departing." In his chapter on Mount Shasta in *Picturesque California* he would call for making the region a national park, "for the welfare and benefit of all mankind, preserving its fountains and forests and all its glad life in primeval beauty."

Because Muir was not in good health, they made much of the trip by train, against his wishes. The food he ate on the train upset his stomach so badly that Keith would not let him climb Mount Hood, in Oregon, telling him he was too ill. But Muir would not be stopped when they reached Seattle, Washington, on August 8, with glistening, glacier-covered Mount Rainier nearby. He agreed that he was not strong enough to go all the way to the summit, but he meant to climb at least to the mountain's flank.

With six companions whom they met in Seattle they started the ascent on the morning of August 9. Muir had stomach troubles again, for something they had eaten the night before had made everyone sick—"There was poison and sickness in every pot," he declared—and he was green-faced and somber as they set out. But once they were camped at Paradise Valley, a third of the way up Rainier's side, his mood changed. There above him lay the splendid peak, "wholly unveiled, awful in bulk and majesty, filling all the view like a separate, new-born world," and he knew he would have to conquer it.

After five days exploring the lower reaches of the mountain, Muir and six of the others began the climb to the summit on August 14. At fifty, he was the oldest in the party, and he had recently been ill, yet his muscles had lost none of their spring, and he moved with agility along the steep, gravel-strewn paths, helping the others through the most difficult places. The wind was strong and cold, and rocks occasionally came bounding down from crumbling ledges. The last stretch was a scramble in steel-nailed shoes over a shining glacier. About a thousand feet from the top one of the climbers, a teen-age boy named Booth, cried out that he could go no farther. The other six left him there to await their return. By noon, after seven and a half hours of climbing, they reached the summit. One of the climbers began taking photographs—the first time a camera had been used at such an altitude, 14,400 feet above sea level. Muir sat silent, peering out at the mighty Cascade Range. After two hours, his keen eyes caught sight of an approaching storm, and he suggested they descend. Just as they started down, Booth came gasping up to join them; he had struggled on to the top after all.

Skidding and bounding, they rushed down, "heart and limb exultant and free." Muir's spirit soared; he had returned to his icy peaks, and they had not rejected him. That night he wrote to Louie, "Did not mean to climb it, but got excited, and soon was on top." Then, as his companions slept, he went out to stroll by himself in the dark forest.

She was writing to him, too. When he reached Seattle again a few days later, he found a letter from her that said, "A ranch that needs and takes the sacrifice of a noble life, or work, ought to be flung away beyond all reach and power for harm. . . . The

Alaska book and the Yosemite book, dear John, must be written, and you need to be your own self, well and strong, to make them worthy of you. There is nothing that has a right to be considered beside this except the welfare of our children."

12

Muir the Crusader

By the end of 1888 John Muir and his wife agreed that the time had come to break free from the ranch, which had drained so much of his energy. He had put aside enough money to support him for the rest of his life; now he should be devoting himself entirely to exploration and research, to the writing of books, and to the campaign to preserve the wilderness.

But he could not have his freedom overnight. First he had to find someone to buy or lease the ranch or, at the least, a capable foreman to run it in his name. And he still had much work to do on the huge volumes of *Picturesque California,* an assignment he bitterly regretted having taken. One responsibility conflicted with the other. In order to be done with his editing chores, he left the ranch and its distracting demands for several months in the summer of 1889, taking a room in San Francisco's Palace Hotel and spending many hours a day writing. During this time he told his friend of university days, Professor Butler, that he would "go out only for meals, and peg away awkwardly and laboriously until the wee sma' hours or thereabouts, working long and hard and accomplishing little."

While Muir was engaged in this high-tension literary work, he was visited at his hotel by an editor from New York: Robert Underwood Johnson of the *Century Magazine,* formerly known as *Scribner's.* Johnson had come to San Francisco to round up material on the gold rush of 1849, but he also hoped to tempt Muir into writing for him once again. They talked a bit at the hotel, and then Muir suggested that they adjourn to Yosemite Valley for a few days.

It was a depressing outing. The meadows and Sierra foothills were in gorgeous bloom, Muir wrote to Louie, "and the sugar pines seemed nobler than ever. Indeed, all seems so new I fancy I could take up the study of these mountain glories with fresh enthusiasm as if I were getting into a sort of second youth. . . ." But the valley itself, run by a commission of indifferent politicians appointed by the governor of California, was a "hog-pen." The owners of the hotels and stables in it had plowed up the meadows and cut down the trees to make hayfields for horses, mules, sheep, cows, and pigs. Higher in the Sierra, whole forests had been logged away, so that the forest floor was "bare as the streets of San Francisco," Muir said, while the damage done by sheep was immense: Vast areas had been "trampled and eaten out of existence by hoofed locusts."

Amid this scene of ruination, Robert Underwood Johnson suggested that he and Muir combine forces to save the Sierra Nevada, through an alliance of Muir's eloquence and the *Century*'s prestige and influence. If Muir would do two articles for the magazine, describing the beauties of the Yosemite region and calling for the creation of a Yosemite National Park, Johnson would enlist the aid of powerful Eastern leaders to make the park a reality. Muir was skeptical, remembering the quick death of the two park bills of 1881, but he agreed to cooperate.

First he finished *Picturesque California,* which kept him busy into the winter of 1889-90. Then he settled down to design some national parks. At that time there was only one such park, Yellowstone, established by Congress in 1872 as "a public park or pleasuring-ground for the benefit and enjoyment of the people," with a pledge of provision for "the preservation, from injury or spoliation, of all timber, mineral deposits, natural curiosities or wonders . . . and their retention in their natural condition." Muir felt the same kind of protection should be extended to Yosemite. Congress had given Yosemite Valley to California in 1864, and Muir, though he disapproved strongly of the way the state was handling things there, saw no hope of getting the valley back under federal control because of the political problems involved. But he found no reason why the state-owned valley could not be surrounded by a much larger park under federal administration, a park which "should at least comprehend all the basins of the streams that pour into the valley."

On March 4, 1890, he sent Johnson a map he had drawn outlining a projected Yosemite National Park. It took in the Merced and Tuolumne river basins, including Hetch Hetchy Valley, and three groves of giant sequoias, the Mariposa Grove among them. He also designed a national park to the south, in the Kings River region, that would encompass most of the other important sequoia groves.

Two weeks later, Representative William Vandever offered Congress a Yosemite Park bill based on Muir's ideas, but omitting much of the northern part of Muir's proposed park. To Muir this was not nearly satisfactory. "As I have urged over and over again," he wrote to Johnson on May 8, "the Yosemite Reservation ought to include all the Yosemite fountains. They all lie in a compact mass of mountains that are glorious scenery, easily accessible from the grand Yosemite center, and are not valuable for any other use than the use of beauty." Johnson went before the House Committee on Public Lands to read Muir's statements and urge the extension of the suggested national park as far north as the Tuolumne Basin and as far east as the Nevada boundary. This meant a fivefold expansion of the Vandever proposal: from 288 to 1,512 square miles.

Muir, meanwhile, was hard at work on his articles for the *Century*. They were major essays, many thousands of words long, and by the time he finished them in early June he was exhausted, underweight, and suffering from a bronchial cough. He suggested his usual prescription for himself: a camping trip among the Alaskan glaciers. A doctor warned him that if he went on the journey in his present condition, he would pay for it with his life. "If I *don't* go," Muir replied, "I'll pay for it with my life."

He sailed for Seattle on June 14. Soon his cough disappeared and his appetite became ferocious. By early July he was camped at Glacier Bay, Alaska, and on July 11 he set out on one of his greatest adventures—a ten-day sled trip across the mighty back of Muir Glacier. Although he had traveled north with a few friends, none of them cared to risk the glacier trek, and so, as usual, he went forth from camp alone.

His sled, which he had made himself, weighed about 100 pounds when fully loaded with food and scientific equipment. He hauled it up the side of the glacier and jauntily embarked into a frozen world where no man had ever gone before. Winds and occasional snow gave him no difficulties, though he had an uneasy moment in a place he named Howling Valley, when, while eating his breakfast, he "heard the dismal long-drawn-out howl of a wolf, soon answered by another and another at greater distances and at short intervals coming nearer and nearer, indicating that they had discovered me and were coming down the mountain to observe me more closely, or perhaps to attack me. . . ." Local Indians had warned Muir of these fierce wolves, which they considered more dangerous than bears. As a matter of philosophy, he had never carried a gun on any of his wanderings since his earliest Yosemite days; the best he could do now was take shelter behind a large boulder on the glacier and prepare to defend himself with his ice ax. But the wolves did not challenge him.

A few days later, descending a 3,000-foot-high mountain he called Snow Dome, he decided to save himself some steps by sliding down a smooth, snow-lined groove in the ice. Down he glided in an easy, comfortable swish until he struck a rough spot. "There I suddenly lost control of myself," he wrote, "and went rolling and bouncing like a boulder until stopped by plashing into the loose gravelly delta." A little groggy, he came slowly to his senses at the bottom and was startled by the weird, piercing cries of two ravens who had swooped toward him, "impatiently waiting for bone-picking time." Muir shook his fist at them and called, "Not yet!"

Toward the middle of the glacier he came to a zone of numerous crevasses, but these were no problem for him after his feats with Stickeen nine years before. He crossed them, sled and all, and sat down on the far side to enjoy his customary lunch, a crust of bread: "To dine with a glacier on a sunny day is a glorious thing and makes common feasts of meat and wine ridiculous." In the evening, after brewing some tea, he settled into his sleeping bag, but not to sleep; at midnight he was still filling his notebook: "Solemn loveliness of the night. Vast star-garden of the Universe. . . . In this silent, serene wilderness the weary gain a heart-bath in perfect peace."

His cough was entirely gone—"no microbe could survive in this icy world"—but there were other troubles as he went along. His shoes were wearing out, and his feet, still lame from the freezing of 1875 on Mount Shasta, were in constant pain. The glare of sunlight reflected from the ice fields gave him a bad case of snowblindness. And on his next-to-last day he plunged through a thin icy crust into a water-filled crevasse, nearly drowning, and pulling himself out so soaked that he came close to freezing as he "shivered the night away." Still, he managed a cheery Scots phrase for his notebook: *"It micht hae been waur!"* It might have been worse!

He was home in September, 1890, after one of the finest exploits of his life, a remarkable accomplishment for a fifty-two-year-old man who had been in poor health. His two *Century* articles, "Treasures of the Yosemite" and "Features of the Proposed Yosemite National Park," had now been published and he found a furious debate raging. Easterners were bombarding Congress with letters and telegrams demanding that the parks Muir advocated be created. But Westerners, still more concerned with profit than with conservation, generally opposed the idea of putting so much land forever beyond the reach of miners, loggers, and herdsmen. Newspaper articles denounced the park plan as a plot to rob California of its most prized possession, as though Yosemite Valley were going to be moved to some other state. Muir himself came under attack. An Oakland politician, John P. Irish, declared that before Muir had "abandoned himself to profitable rhapsody and became a pseudo-naturalist," he had himself been one of the exploiters and despoilers of Yosemite: "There he cut and logged and sawed the trees of the Valley with as willing a hand as any lumberman in the Sierras. When the State of California became trustee of the grant, Muir and the mill were expelled . . . and his teeth have been on edge ever since. The State got there, however, in time to save the forests from Mr. Muir's lumbering operations, and to prevent the clogging of the Merced with sawdust, to the destruction of its beauty and its trout." Though Muir had never troubled to reply to his critics, this was so incredible a distortion that he could not remain silent, and on September 14 he wrote to the Oakland *Tribune* to assert that he had logged only fallen timber in the valley: "I never cut down a single tree in the Yosemite, nor sawed a tree cut down by any other person there. Furthermore, I never held, or tried to hold any sort of claim in the valley, or sold a foot of lumber there or elsewhere."

As the battle for the national parks reached its climax, the conservationist forces acquired an odd ally: the Southern Pacific Railroad. Though the trainmen had done more than their share of destruction of the environment, running tracks through virgin forests so that their smoke-belching locomotives could pass, they recognized that creation of these parks would greatly stimulate tourism in California, to their advantage. Therefore, the railroad lobbyists added their influential voices to those of John Muir and Robert Underwood

Johnson. On September 25, 1890, Congress passed a bill creating Sequoia National Park, extending across the whole basin of the Kaweah River and removing much of Muir's Giant Forest from the perils of logging. A few days later, Congress set up another national park nearby: General Grant National Park, taking in the Grant Grove of giant sequoias. (Since 1940 this has been part of Kings Canyon National Park.) And on October 1 the law establishing Yosemite National Park won approval. The park that was finally created was almost identical in boundaries to the one that John Muir had proposed seven months before.

This great triumph for Muir was followed almost at once by sadness: At the end of October his father-in-law, Dr. Strentzel, died. Now the full management of the ranch fell to Muir, while Louie was required to spend much of her time caring for her mother. These burdens were eased somewhat in the spring of 1891, when Muir's sister Maggie and her husband, John Reid, came to live at the ranch. The Reids had owned a farm in Nebraska but had incurred heavy losses on account of drought and had given up. Now Muir was able to turn many of the ranch responsibilities over to his brother-in-law.

His newest project was the extension of Sequoia National Park to include the Kings Canyon region. Secretary of the Interior John W. Noble was sympathetic to the idea and asked Muir to draw a map of his proposed park expansion. In May, 1891, Muir revisited Kings Canyon, drew his map, and gathered material for a *Century* article he called "A Rival of the Yosemite." It ended with the words "This region contains no mines of consequence; it is too high and too rocky for agriculture, and even the lumber industry need suffer no unreasonable restriction. Let our lawgivers then make haste, before it is too late, to save this surpassingly glorious region for the recreation and well-being of humanity, and the world will rise up and call them blessed."

The lawgivers, however, were not interested in expanding the national parks just then. But Secretary Noble did manage to slip one valuable piece of legislation through Congress in 1891. It allowed the President to set aside by proclamation, without special act of Congress, any publicly owned lands that were covered with timber, designating them as forest reservations. Under the terms of this act President Benjamin Harrison set aside 13,000,000 acres of land, notably the Sierra Forest Reserve—4,000,000 acres in California, beginning at the southern boundary of Yosemite National Park and stretching south far enough to take in the entire belt of giant sequoias. This decree did not give the region full protection—500,000 sheep a year continued to graze there—but at least the world's biggest trees now were safe from loggers.

Muir by now had emerged as the Western leader of the conservationist movement, and an organization had formed around him. In 1889, Robert Underwood Johnson had urged him to "start an association for preserving California's monuments and natural wonders—or at least Yosemite." Muir, the eternal loner, did not have much faith in organizations, but he did discuss the idea with a few of his friends, and by late 1890 or early 1891 serious plans for such an association were being drawn up, under the name of the Sierra Club. Its official existence dates from May 28, 1892, when Muir and about two dozen associates brought the Sierra Club into being in a lawyer's office in San Francisco. He was unanimously chosen its president, a post he would hold for the rest of his life.

The Sierra Club's incorporation papers stated its purposes as, first, "To explore, enjoy, and render accessible the mountain regions of the Pacific Coast" and "to publish authentic information concerning them," and then "to enlist the support and cooperation of the people and the government in preserving the forests and other natural features of the Sierra Nevada Mountains." Its membership, which grew rapidly, included some who were primarily lovers of mountains and mountaineering and some whose main interest was conservation. In John Muir, of course, these two interests were equally represented.

There was immediate work for the Sierra Club. In February, 1892, Representative Anthony Caminetti of California introduced in Congress a bill that would have cut Yosemite National Park in half, once again opening large areas to grazing, mining, and logging. Muir, when he learned of this attempt to undo the good work of 1890, spoke out sharply against it in newspaper interviews, and the Sierra Club sent formal notice of its opposition to Congress. Thanks to these protests, Yosemite National Park escaped mutilation, although Caminetti sponsored several similar bills in the next few years. The watchfulness of the Sierra Club brought about their defeat, and in 1894 Caminetti failed to be reelected to Congress. But there would be other attempts to reduce the park's size.

Muir had almost entirely retired now from management of the ranch. He spent much of his time in San Francisco, handling the affairs of the Sierra Club and visiting with his many friends. Perhaps the closest of these was the painter William Keith, who had climbed many mountains with him in quest of striking scenery. Keith and Muir had often talked of making a European tour together, but they never could schedule the trip. Abruptly, in May, 1893, Keith sent his friend a telegram: "I can't wait any longer. I'm starting tomorrow." Muir instantly dropped all his work and started to pack. He reached San Francisco a couple of days later, but found Keith already gone, leaving behind a message saying he would meet Muir in Chicago. Muir set out after him, stopping only in Wisconsin to visit his mother. In Chicago, though, he found another note from Keith: "Couldn't stand the crowd. Will wait in New York."

"The crowd" Keith meant was the horde of visitors to the Chicago World's Columbian Exposition. Muir toured it before continuing eastward. It was, he wrote to Louie, a "rat's nest, containing much rubbish and commonplace stuff as well as things novel and precious." He most enjoyed the art galleries, "about eighteen acres of paintings by every nation under the sun," where he "wandered and gazed until I was ready to fall down with utter exhaustion." Four paintings by Keith were on display, but "not his best." At night the fairgrounds were stunning: "The buildings and terraces and fountains along the canals were illuminated by tens of thousands of electric lights arranged along miles of lines of gables, domes, and cornices, with glorious effect." Large-scale electric lighting was still something fairly new, and Muir, for all his love of natural wonders, was awed by this man-made spectacle: "It was all fairyland on a colossal scale and would have made the Queen of Sheba and poor Solomon in all their glory feel sick with helpless envy."

On May 30 he reached New York, where he had spent such a harried visit twenty-five years before. He found Keith, who was involved in a round of receptions put on in his honor by the leaders of society and the art world. Muir too was rapidly subjected to the celebrity treatment. His editor, Robert Underwood Johnson, took him in tow and whirled him through banquets, speaking engagements, private dinners with millionaires, and so forth. Muir would have preferred to shut himself in his hotel room and write, but, he reported to Louie, Johnson "quietly ordered me around and took possession of me," plunging him into a frenzy of "new people, visits, dinners, champagne, etc." Wherever he went he was the center of attention: "I had no idea I was so well known, considering the little I have written," he said with what probably was sincere modesty. He found that everyone wanted to hear his Stickeen story. "I must have told it at least twelve times," he wrote on June 13.

Johnson took him on a side trip to Boston. He went from there to Concord, where he had dinner with Ralph Waldo Emerson's son and made a sentimental pilgrimage to the old philosopher's grave. It was marked not by an ordinary tombstone but by a mass of white quartz bearing no inscription. "It seems to have been dropped there by a glacier," Muir commented, "and the soil he sleeps in is glacial drift almost wholly unchanged since first this country saw the light at the close of the glacial period." Nearby were the graves of two others cherished by Muir: Henry David Thoreau and Nathaniel Hawthorne. When he left the cemetery, Muir walked through the woods to Thoreau's Walden Pond, which he found extraordinarily beautiful: "No wonder Thoreau lived here two years. I could have enjoyed living here two hundred years or two thousand." That evening he met an old man who had been Thoreau's schoolmate and lifelong friend. "The old gentleman kept his seat and seemed, I thought, a little cold and careless in his manner," Muir told Louie. "But when Johnson said, 'This is Mr. Muir,' he jumped up and said excitedly, 'John Muir! Is this John Muir?' and seized me as if I were a long-lost son. He declared he had known me always, and that my name was a household word."

Then he returned to New York for more "grand dinners, formal and informal, and here I told my dog story, I don't know how often, and described glaciers and their works." He was introduced to another famous naturalist, John Burroughs, as well as to Mark Twain and Rudyard Kipling. He bore up well under the strain, observing, "Last night another champagne supper, and another tonight. But my stomach . . . behaves like a gentleman." It was a relief, though, when he finally boarded his ship for Europe on June 26. Keith, having lost patience with all the banqueting, had sailed on June 3, and though they intended to meet on the other side, they never did.

Muir reached England in early July and went at once to Scotland, touring the city of Edinburgh in the company of David Douglas, a book publisher to whom Robert Underwood Johnson had given him a letter of introduction. "From feeling lonely and a stranger in my own native land," Muir said, "he brought me back into quick and living contact with it, and now I am a Scotchman and at home again." He went on to his hometown, Dunbar, sauntering its streets, visiting his childhood home, looking up old playmates. "I remember it pretty well," he wrote to his seven-year-old daughter Helen, "and the school where the teacher used to whip me so much, though I tried to be good all the time and learn my lessons." To twelve-year-old Wanda he wrote of walking "along the shore on the rocks where I played when a boy. The waves made a grand show breaking in sheets and sheaves of foam, and grand songs, the same old songs they sang to me in my childhood, and I seemed a boy again. . . ."

Then he was off to Norway, to glacial fjords and valleys that reminded him of Yosemite, and then back to England for an extensive tour, and then to Switzerland and the mighty Alps. He was tempted to climb the almost unclimbable Matterhorn, "a huge savage pyramid . . . piercing the heavens in lonely serene majesty," but he knew the task was now beyond his strength. Looking up at white-mantled Mont Blanc two days later, "it was hard to hold my legs back, sick or well, old or young," but he resisted the urge. On he went across Switzerland, examining the rocks and glaciers that had inspired the theories of Louis Agassiz, into Italy. Then he returned to England once more to see the sights of London, and crossed over to Ireland for a view of lovely bogs and lakes. After final visits to Edinburgh and Dunbar he sailed for New York on September 16, 1893.

A telegram from Louie awaited him there, suggesting that he stop in Washington before coming home and confer with officials of the new administration of President Cleveland on conservationist matters. He did this, meeting with Secretary of the Interior Hoke Smith and several other Cabinet members and Senators.

There was a winter of hard work in store for him in California. Though he had been a professional writer for more than twenty years, he had never published a book of his own. He had to his credit only the two volumes of *Picturesque California,* most of which had been written by others and merely edited by John Muir. But now Robert Underwood Johnson had persuaded him to put together some of his old Sierra essays in a book called *The Mountains of California.*

He took the assignment seriously. On April 3, 1894, he notified Johnson that the book "is finished and out of me, therefore hurrah, etc., and thanks to you, very friend, for benevolent prodding. Six of the sixteen chapters are new, and the others are nearly so, for I have worked hard on every one of them, leaning them against each other, adding lots of new stuff, and killing adjectives and adverbs of redundant growth—the *verys, intenses, gloriouses, ands,* and *buts,* by the score." What emerged was his finest prose: as vivid and imaginative as ever, but stripped of unnecessary ornament and overstatement. The book was published that autumn and met with immediate success. Its glowing words inspired many to lend their support to Muir's campaign to save the Western forests.

Johnson promptly asked him to do a second book, on Yosemite alone. Muir used this as a pretext to revisit the Sierra in the summer of 1895. Alone, as in the old days, carrying no gun, no blanket, and only bread and tea by way of provisions, he roamed the wild country of the Tuolumne Basin in total delight. "I suppose old age will put an end to scrambling in rocks and ice," he wrote to his mother, "but I can still climb as well as ever." To Louie he wrote of meeting a great many bears in Hetch Hetchy Valley, "but they gave no trouble, as I knew they wouldn't. Only in tangled underbrush I had to shout a good deal to avoid coming suddenly on them." He was pleased to see how the vegetation was recovering everywhere in the park, now that government soldiers prohibited sheepmen from grazing their flocks in it. But the Yosemite Valley, still under California administration in the midst of the national park, was a depressing sight: "Dusty, downtrodden, abandoned, and pathetic," he told Johnson. "It looks ten times worse now than when you saw it seven years ago. Most of the level meadow floor of the valley is fenced with barbed and unbarbed wire and about three hundred head of horses are turned loose every night to feed and trample the flora out of existence. I told the hotel and horsemen that they were doing all they could to prevent lovers of wild beauties from visiting the valley. . . . As long as the management [of the valley] is in the hands of eight politicians appointed by the ever-changing Governor of California, there is but little hope." He recommended to the Sierra Club that a campaign to bring about the transfer of Yosemite Valley to the national government be launched.

13

Elder Statesman

Whenever a crisis in conservationist affairs arose, it was now customary to turn to John Muir. He had become the elder statesman of the conservationist cause. It was strange, then, that he was not appointed to the National Forestry Commission that President Cleveland created in 1896 to survey the country's forest reserves and recommend a permanent natural-resources policy. But in fact, Muir preferred not to accept appointment to this commission, asking rather that he be associated with it as a free-lance adviser. He would accompany the six commissioners on their reconnaissance of the Western forests, but he was too weary to travel throughout the entire country, as they intended to do.

The commissioners were able ones. Their chairman was Charles Sargent, a Harvard botanist. The other members were William Brewer of Yale, a geologist; General H. L. Abbott, an engineer; Arnold Hague of the U.S. Geological Survey; Gifford Pinchot, an authority on forestry; and Alexander

Agassiz of Harvard, son of Louis Agassiz and a distinguished zoologist in his own right. They began a survey of the forest resources of the Middle West in the spring of 1896. Muir, at home in the Alhambra Valley, continued with his writing.

One June morning he was possessed by another of his strange intuitions: "The idea that I ought to go back to Portage, Wisconsin, to see my mother once more, as she was not likely to live long, though I had not heard that she was failing." As before, he had total faith in his impulse and hurried to his mother's home, sending telegrams along the way to his brother Dan and his sister Mary in Nebraska. He sent no word to Wisconsin, however, and when he made his sudden appearance there his sister Sarah, spying him through the front window, cried out in surprise, "Why, there's John!" She ran to him, exclaiming, "God must have sent you, because mother is very sick." Indeed she seemed close to death. Six of the Muir children gathered at her bedside, though, and she appeared to rally. She grew so strong, in fact, that John Muir believed she was out of danger, and he went on to Harvard, where he had been invited to speak at the graduation ceremonies on June 24. The day before the commencement exercises he received word that his mother had died in her sleep. He gave his speech, received an honorary degree of Master of Arts, and returned to Wisconsin for her funeral.

As long as he had crossed the continent, he chose now to meet the members of the National Forestry Commission in Chicago and go westward with them.

They went first to the pine forests of South Dakota's Black Hills, where they discovered large areas stripped bare by mining activities and illegal logging. "Wherever the white man goes, the groves vanish," Muir wrote home. In Wyoming and Montana, too, wasteful forest practices had left immense zones of devastation. The forests of Washington and Oregon were also under attack, and in the redwood country of northern California's coast they found "the work of ruin going on," with large tracts transformed into "a desolate rugged expanse of black stumps." Muir left the commissioners there, but they went on to Arizona, where they observed the destruction of the forests surrounding the Grand Canyon and the harmful effects of mining operations within the canyon itself.

Muir helped write the commission's report, which was placed before President Cleveland in February, 1897. It urged the repeal of the laws under which private interests were allowed to exploit the natural resources of publicly owned land and called for the scientific management of forests to maintain a permanent timber supply. In addition, it recommended the creation of two new national parks, Grand Canyon and Mount Rainier, and called upon the President to set aside thirteen new forest reserves, totaling 21,000,000 acres, in eight Western states. President Cleveland, whose term of office was due to expire in another few weeks, could do nothing about the two new national parks, but on February 22 he celebrated the hundred and sixty-fifth anniversary of George Washington's birth by proclaiming the thirteen forest reserves.

The outcries from mining companies, lumbermen, and herdsmen were vehement and vociferous. To men who had grown rich by tapping the public domain, it seemed outrageous that so much potentially valuable land would be put away beyond their reach. They bombarded Congress with protests, and in the closing days of Cleveland's term a band of angry Western Senators showed their displeasure by trying to impeach him. But there was no need to go that far. On March 4, 1897, Cleveland left the White House and was replaced by William McKinley, who was much more sympathetic to the desires of big business. McKinley's Secretary of the Interior, Cornelius N. Bliss, kept the National Forestry Commission's report from being made public, so that the citizenry would not learn of the damage being done to the forests. Congress voted in the spring to suspend President Cleveland's forest-reserve decree until March 1, 1898. Then Bliss ruled that mining speculators and loggers could file claims on the land covered by that decree until it actually went into effect. Naturally, there was a stampede to secure chunks of public forest in the nine months before private claims would be banned.

The California forest reserves were not affected by these steps, thanks to the insistence of the two California Senators, who would not let that land be reopened for exploitation. But Congress' action was nevertheless a strong blow against the conservationists. "This forest battle," Muir declared, "is part of the eternal conflict between right and wrong. . . . The sooner it is stirred up and debated before the people the better, for thus the light will be let into it." To Robert Underwood Johnson he wrote, "Those western corporations with their shady millions seem invincible in the Senate. *But the fight must go on!"*

Through newspaper interviews, through letters to powerful friends in Washington, and through statements from the Sierra Club, Muir worked to mobilize public opinion. He contributed passionate articles to every major national magazine. The most eloquent of these was "American Forests," in the August, 1897, issue of the *Atlantic Monthly.* It opened with a description of the great American forests as they had been in the days when Indians alone inhabited the continent: "But when the steel axe of the white man rang out on the startled air their doom was sealed. Every tree heard the bodeful sound, and pillars of smoke gave a sign in the sky."

He went on, "Every other civilized nation in the world has been compelled to care for its forests." But the United States, "like a rich and foolish spendthrift," had allowed its heritage "to be sold and plundered and wasted at will." Who were the opponents of the forest-reserve plan, Muir asked? They were "thieves who are wealthy and steal timber by wholesale. They have so long been allowed to steal and destroy in peace that any impediment to forest robbery is denounced as a cruel and irreligious interference with 'vested rights.' " Congressmen, he implied, had been bought by private interests: "Even in Congress, a sizable chunk of gold, carefully concealed, will outtalk and outfight all the nation on a subject like forestry." He ended the piece with these blazing words:

"Any fool can destroy trees. They cannot run away; and if they could, they would still be destroyed—chased and hunted down as long as fun or a dollar could be got out of their bark hides, branching horns, or magnificent bole backbones. Few that fell trees plant them; nor would planting avail much towards getting back anything like the noble primeval forests. During a man's life only saplings can be grown, in the place of the old trees—tens of centuries old—that have been destroyed. It took more than three thousand years to make some of the trees in these western woods—trees that are still standing in perfect strength and beauty, waving and singing in the mighty forests of the Sierra. Through all the wonderful, eventful centuries since Christ's time—and long before that—God has cared for these trees, saved them from drought, disease, avalanches, and a thousand straining, leveling tempests and floods; but He cannot save them from fools—only Uncle Sam can do that."

On March 1, 1898, the temporary suspension of President Cleveland's decree came to an end. The Senate now voted to abolish the forest reserves altogether, throwing millions of acres open to private use. But the House of Representatives, heeding

Muir's appeal, defeated this proposal by a vote of 100 to 39. The forest reserves were saved.

When not involved in conservationist battles, Muir continued his travels. In the summer of 1897 he paid a brief visit to Alaska, where he witnessed the "grand, splattering, jostling, floundering onrush" of men on their way to the Yukon River to take part in the Klondike gold rush. He called the scene "a wild discouraging mess." A year later he toured the hills of North Carolina and Tennessee with two botanist friends, Charles Sargent and William Canby. He had been ill again with grippe and a bronchial cough, and told Sargent, "I don't want to die without once more saluting the grand, godly, round-headed trees of the east side of America that I first learned to love and beneath which I used to weep for joy when nobody knew me." After a few days of hiking he reported to Louie, "The air has healed me," and said, "I think I could walk ten miles and not be tired." Having retraced much of his old route of 1867, he went on to Boston and New York, and, late in 1898, went down to Florida with Sargent. In the town of Cedar Key he looked for the Hodgsons, who had nursed him back to health when he was ill with malaria more than thirty years before. Mr. Hodgson had died long ago, but his wife and children still were there. "I found the good old lady who nursed me," he told Louie. "I asked her if she knew me. She answered no, and asked my name. I said Muir. '*John* Muir?' she almost screamed. '*My* California John Muir? My California John?' I said, 'Why, yes, I promised to come back and visit you in about twenty-five years, and though a little late I've come.' "

Homesickness sent him back to California by Christmas. But in the spring of 1899 he was off again—to Alaska once more, as the guest of the railroad millionaire E. H. Harriman. This great tycoon had invited some two dozen scientists to sail with him, including William H. Brewer, who had been a member of the National Forestry Commission, and John Burroughs, whose fame as a naturalist rivaled Muir's. Among the others in the group were Henry Gannett, chief geographer of the U.S. Geological Survey, and C. Hart Merriam, head of the U.S. Biological Survey. Harriman's ship, the *George W. Elder,* was outfitted as a floating laboratory for the use of these distinguished scientists. The expedition numbered 126 altogether, including Harriman's wife and 5 children. (The youngest of the five, eight-year-old Averell, would one day serve as a Cabinet member, as American ambassador to Russia and Great Britain, and as governor of New York.)

Muir thoroughly enjoyed himself in this company, though he was often the victim of the sharp wit of his longtime correspondent John Burroughs. "In John Muir we had an authority on glaciers," Burroughs wrote, "and a thorough one—so thorough that he would not allow the rest of the party to have an opinion on the subject." When some members of the expedition went on a hunting trip across the Muir Glacier and failed to find the wolves that had worried Muir in Howling Valley, Burroughs commented that there might not ever have been any wolves there—"Muir's imagination may have done all the howling." But such quips, and there were many of them, were aimed in a good-natured way.

Muir himself got off the best line of all at his host's expense. During a discussion of Harriman's wealth, Muir suddenly said, "Why, I am richer than Harriman. I have all the money I want, and he hasn't." When Harriman heard the story, he went to Muir and said, "I never cared for money except as power for work. . . . What I most enjoy is the power of creation, getting into partnership with Nature in doing good, helping to feed man and beast, and making everybody and everything a little better and happier." To Muir he sounded sincere. Muir had a natural distaste for millionaires, especially for those who had made their money by building railroads across the wilderness, and he had begun the voyage feeling "rather repelled" by the cold, aloof Harriman. But by its end, he said, "I at last learned to love him." His only serious disagreement with the magnate came over Harriman's fondness for hunting. One of Harriman's main purposes in making the trip was to shoot a Kodiak bear, the largest of carnivorous land animals, and eventually he succeeded in this. Muir noted bitterly in his journal, "Harriman returned last evening after killing two bears—mother and child."

At the age of sixty-one Muir found that he could climb as well as ever, and he scampered with his usual enthusiasm across glaciers and up mountains.

As often as he could he left the comforts of the ship to go on camping trips on the icy Alaskan shore. In Glacier Bay he observed that the Muir Glacier had retreated two miles since he first had seen it twenty years before. In a fjord near Prince William Sound he and the geologist Henry Gannett camped overnight at the edge of a hemlock forest, pitying those who were enjoying a shipboard party. When the *Elder* later sailed past Taylor Bay, Muir left another party to stand alone by the rail, looking out toward the glacier where he and Stickeen had had their unforgettable adventure.

The two-month voyage was far less arduous than any of his past journeys, but despite himself, he enjoyed the novelty of traveling in ease. Back at home at the end of August, 1899, he wrote a thank-you note to the Harriman daughters in which he said, "No doubt every one of the favored happy band feels, as I do, that this was the grandest trip of his life. To me it was peculiarly grateful and interesting because nearly all my life I have wandered and studied alone. On the *Elder,* I found not only the fields I liked best to study, but a hotel, a club, and a home, together with a floating university in which I enjoyed the instruction and companionship of a lot of the best fellows imaginable. . . ."

For a while, now, Muir lived quietly at home, working on his second book. He had put aside his proposed Yosemite book and instead was assembling and revising a group of his magazine articles into a volume called *Our National Parks,* which was published in 1901. There now were five such parks, for to Yellowstone and the 1890 trio of Yosemite, Sequoia, and General Grant had been added Mount Rainier, in 1899. After discussing these, Muir turned to other wilderness regions that he felt deserved the same protection, observing that "while protective measures are being deliberated languidly, destruction and use are speeding on faster and farther every day. The axe and saw are insanely busy, chips are flying thick as snowflakes, and every summer thousands of acres of priceless forests, with their underbrush, soil, springs, climate, scenery, and religion, are vanishing away in clouds of smoke, while, except in the national parks, not one forest guard is employed."

The conservationist cause gained a mighty ally in September, 1901, when Theodore Roosevelt became President following the assassination of McKinley. In his first message to Congress, three months later, he declared that preservation of the forests was "an imperative business necessity," and said, "The forest and water problems are perhaps the most vital internal questions of the United States at the present time." He proposed strict regulations to keep sheep and other livestock out of the forest reserves and called for the creation of a Bureau of Forestry under the Department of Agriculture. Then in 1902 he and his Secretary of the Interior, Ethan Allen Hitchcock, opened war on the "malefactors of great wealth" who had used fraudulent means to gain possession of public land in the West.

In March, 1903, John Muir learned that President Roosevelt was planning to visit California shortly and was eager to go hiking in the Sierra with Muir as his guide. Muir had made plans of his own to tour the forests of Japan, Russia, and China that spring; but the opportunity to make his views on forestry and national parks known to the President was too good to pass up, and he postponed the date of his departure. "I do not want anyone with me but you," Roosevelt wrote him, "and I want to drop politics absolutely for four days, and just be out in the open with you."

The President arrived in San Francisco in May. On May 14, the night before the Sierra trip was due to start, Muir presented himself at the Palace Hotel, where a reception in Roosevelt's honor was in progress. It seemed likely to go on all night, and Muir, announcing that he was tired and wanted to go to bed, left the hotel without seeing the President, taking the ferry across to Oakland where the Presidential train was waiting. Not for a President or any man would he lose his sleep, he said. Roosevelt was charmed by Muir's brusque and stubborn individuality when they finally met, the next morning.

By the evening of the fifteenth Muir and Roosevelt were camped out under the giant sequoias of Mariposa Grove; no one was with them except two park rangers and a cook, who took care to keep out of the way while the President and the naturalist discussed the forestry problem. Muir did most of the talking. "I stuffed him pretty well," he said later, "regarding the timber thieves, and the destructive work of the lumbermen, and other spoilers of the forests." The next day Muir and Roosevelt slipped away from the main party again, taking horses out to Glacier Point, where food had been left for them. He and the President built a campfire and grilled thick steaks for themselves; then they talked until sundown, and when it was dark, Muir quietly went over to a tall dead pine and set it afire, knowing the gaudy display would please Roosevelt. "Hurrah!" the President cried. "That's a candle it took five hundred years to make. Hurrah for Yosemite!" That night, as they camped without tents high above Yosemite Valley, Muir described the valley's squalid condition under California's administration and urged the President to have it returned to federal control. Roosevelt agreed that that should be done.

Muir felt no need to be diplomatic with the President. When Roosevelt began to talk about big-game hunting, one of his favorite hobbies, Muir broke in, saying, "Mr. Roosevelt, when are you going to get beyond the boyishness of killing things? Are you not getting far enough along to leave that off?"

Roosevelt thought a moment and replied, "Muir, I guess you are right." He went on hunting anyway, but did most of his killing for the sake of collecting museum specimens, rather than for sport alone.

The four days Muir spent with Theodore Roosevelt in Yosemite undoubtedly greatly reinforced the President's already strong conservationist philosophy and convinced him of the need for swift action. Immediately after leaving the park, Roosevelt spoke at Sacramento, declaring, "No small part of the prosperity of California in the hotter and drier agricultural regions depends upon the preservation of her water supply; and the water supply cannot be preserved unless the forests are preserved. As regards some of the trees, I want them preserved because they are the only things of their kind in the world. Lying out at night under those giant sequoias was lying in a temple built by no hand of man, a temple grander than any human architect could by any possibility build, and I hope for the preservation of the groves of giant trees simply because it would be a shame to our civilization to let them disappear. . . . I ask for the preservation of other forests on grounds of wise and far-sighted economic policy. . . . I ask that your marvelous natural resources be handed on unimpaired to your posterity. We are not building this country of ours for a day. It is to last through the ages." In the next six years, Roosevelt would set aside 148,000,000 additional acres of forest reserves. During his administration the number of national parks would double, and he would proclaim sixteen "national monuments" where virtually the same protective laws would be in effect as in national parks.

A week after his camping trip with the President, Muir embarked on an astonishing world tour. With Charles Sargent and his son he sailed to Europe, visiting most of the great capitals before crossing into Russia. He darted all over—up to Finland, down to the Black Sea, through the mountains of the Caucasus, eastward to Moscow. The frantic pace and the strange foods made him ill, and he started to lose weight; but in late summer he wrote to Robert Underwood Johnson, "I'm still alive after this most monstrous dose of civilization—London, Paris, Berlin, etc., etc., with their miles of art galleries, museums full of old armor and murder implements. . . . Glad to leave holy Moscow, Kremlin, and all." On August 3 he and the Sargents boarded the train for Siberia. Europe dwindled behind him as he headed for the port of Vladivostok on the Sea of Japan. A short trip into Manchuria ended when he came down with a bad attack of ptomaine poisoning; he returned to Vladivostok seriously ill, weighing only about 90 pounds, keeping himself going on morphine and brandy. But his strength returned as he sailed down the Korean coast toward China. At Shanghai he parted from the Sargents; they wanted to go into the Chinese interior, and he dreamed of seeing India's mighty Himalayas. With the help of officials of an Oriental steamship line owned by his friend Harriman, he arranged a change in his itinerary, and soon he was en route for Calcutta. "I feel all alive with mountains in sight once more," he wrote to his wife.

He went by train to Darjeeling, the Indian resort city at the edge of the Himalayas, and spent several days paying his respects to these mountains, the loftiest in the world. If he had been able to come here thirty years before, he would surely have clambered to their summits, nearly 30,000 feet above sea level; as it was, he had to be content with the view from a distance. Then he moved on across India. He was troubled by the feeling that his daughter Helen was ill, and having learned in the past to trust such intuitions, he came close to cutting short his travels to go home. But in Bombay he cabled Louie, and received a reassuring reply: "All's well." Impulsively, Muir celebrated by purchasing a steamship ticket for Egypt. By November he was out in the desert close by the Nile, inspecting the Sphinx and the Pyramids.

Nor was his odyssey nearly done. Eastward across the Indian Ocean he came once more; Christmas saw him in the heart of an Australian forest. "I am beginning botany all over again," he reported, as he collected specimens of the unfamiliar plant life of the island continent. Then he went to New Zealand, which, like California, impressed him with its great contrasts: subtropical lowlands and glacier-topped mountains. In a raging storm he prowled across the snout of one of Mount Cook's glaciers and was pleased to announce, "I found my feet had not lost their cunning!" Back to Australia, then, for a look at some towering trees which, while huge, did not come close to matching his beloved sequoias, and then he sailed through the Malayan Archipelago and the Philippines to the coast of China. At the port of Canton he found a message from Harriman, inviting him to travel home on one of the ships of his steamship line. Muir accepted and was given a large stateroom in which he could work on the botanical specimens he had accumulated.

And now the route led homeward, though in no great hurry, for there were lengthy stops in Japan and Hawaii. On May 27, 1904, after more than a year of wandering, he reached San Francisco again. His family and friends were amazed at his appearance, for he had gone away thin, pale, and coughing, and he returned tanned and husky, weighing 148 pounds—the heaviest he had ever been. It was just as well that he had grown so much stronger on his global jaunt, for the fiercest struggles of his conservationist career were now about to begin.

14

Battles Won, Battles Lost

The time had come to open the fight for "recession" of Yosemite Valley—the transfer of the valley from state to federal control. By now many Californians agreed with Muir that the state had not done a good job of protecting the valley and that it was best to let it be merged into nationally owned Yosemite National Park. But there were some, including a few leading members of the Sierra Club, who believed that no patriotic Californian could support a movement to deprive his state of control of Yosemite.

By 1904 the Sierra Club was finally unanimous in favor of recession, and it began to take a public stand. William Colby, the club's secretary, drew up a recession bill that was introduced in the California legislature in January, 1905. Muir and Colby made nine trips to the state capital to argue for the bill. On February 2 it passed in the Assembly by a vote of 46 to 19, but then it ran into trouble in the Senate, where a few diehard patriots fought it bitterly. Once again Muir came under attack, one senator accusing him of "despoiling the forest growth in the Yosemite until he was forced to close down his mill." But—with the aid of Harriman and the powerful railroad lobby—the Senate approved recession by a 21-13 vote on February 23. "I am now an experienced lobbyist," Muir wrote to Robert Underwood Johnson. "My political education is complete. . . ."

It still remained for Congress to accept what California was willing to give. This proved complicated. Joseph Cannon, the Speaker of the House, held up the acceptance bill on the grounds that the federal government could not afford a few thousand dollars to put the valley trails and roads into proper shape. Then the bill became entangled in a scheme to lop off a corner of Yosemite National Park so that a railroad line could be built across parkland. One such reduction of the park's boundaries had already passed Congress on February 7, 1905, over the opposition of Muir and the Sierra Club: 542 square miles in the southwestern section had been excluded from the park, and 113 square miles had been added in the north. Now a further reduction of about 40 square miles was under consideration. In the spring of 1906, after nearly a year of debate, there finally emerged a compromise bill, under which only about 15 square miles would be awarded to the railroad and Yosemite Valley would be accepted from California. Congress gave its approval, and President Roosevelt added his signature on June 11, 1906, at last uniting the famous valley with the lands around it under government protection.

Muir had fought every stage of the recession battle despite severe problems at home. Early in 1905, his daughter Helen had fallen ill with pneumonia, and her physician prescribed a year in dry desert air. As soon as she was strong enough to travel, Muir took her and his older daughter, Wanda, to a ranch near Wilcox, Arizona. A few weeks later—in June, 1905—he received word from Louie, who had remained in California, that she had been sick but was "all right now." Immediately afterward came a telegram calling him to her bedside. Muir and Wanda hurried home and found her close to death with a tumor of the lung.

Louie Muir died on August 6, and Muir, deeply shaken, retreated to the desert with his daughters. He found it impossible to write and lived in a sort of daze, stunned and bewildered. "Get out among the mountains and the trees, friend, as soon as you can," Theodore Roosevelt advised him. Helen was healing rapidly in dry Arizona, and Muir began to go with her and Wanda on horseback rides through the bizarre, strangely eroded countryside. On one of these trips he discovered a marvelous "forest" of fossilized trees, millions of years old, transformed by chemical action over an immense span of time into stone of rich hue. This sparked a new interest in him, and he went to California to do research on fossilized trees in the university library. From there he wrote to Helen, "I sit silent and alone from morn til eve in the deeper silence of the enchanted old forests of the coal age. The hours go on neither long or short, glorious for imagination . . . but tough for the old paleontological body nearing 70. There's no fatness in this work—only leanness. . . ." Gradually these studies drew him from his grief, and the Yosemite Valley victory of June, 1906, helped cheer him further, as did Wanda's marriage that same month to a young civil engineer she had met at college. In August, he brought Helen home from the desert, restored to health, and resumed his careers as writer and crusader. Soon he had another triumph to his credit: Learning that the fossilized trees of Arizona were being hauled away by the carload to be sold as souvenirs, he asked Theodore Roosevelt for help, and late in 1906 the President ended the pillage by establishing Petrified Forest National Monument.

Muir had plans now for at least a dozen books. In the past, when friends urged him to write, he told them he could not take time from his fieldwork until he was too old to climb mountains. Although he still could climb, he was aware now that he could not have many years left on earth, and his notebooks overflowed with the raw material of books that he felt he owed the world. But before he was able to get down to serious work, new problems beset him. In the fall of 1907 Helen's health weakened again, and it became necessary for her to return to the desert. Muir built a cabin for her near the town of Daggett, in the Mojave Desert, and hired a nurse and companion for her. Then he went back alone to the empty house on his California ranch—and found himself embroiled in a struggle to save Hetch Hetchy Valley from destruction.

Hetch Hetchy, north of Yosemite Valley in Yosemite National Park, had many devoted admirers who believed it was more beautiful than Yosemite Valley itself. It was not as large as Yosemite, but its proportions were more agreeable, and its meadows, groves, waterfalls, and cliffs had not been spoiled, as those of Yosemite had, by the construction of hotels, stables, and sawmills. Hetch Hetchy Falls was greater in volume than Yosemite Falls, and in the spring its noise could be heard for miles.

"Imagine yourself in Hetch Hetchy," John Muir once wrote. "It is a sunny day in June, the pines sway dreamily, and you are shoulder-deep in grass and flowers. Looking across the valley through beautiful open groves you see a bare granite wall 1,800 feet high rising abruptly out of the green and yellow vegetation and glowing with sunshine, and in front of it the fall, waving like a downy scarf, silver bright, burning with white sun-fire in every fiber. . . . Now observe the marvelous distinctness and delicacy of the various kinds of sun-filled tissue into which the waters are woven. They fly and float and drowse down the face of that grand rock in so leisurely and unconfused a manner that you may examine their texture and patterns as you would a piece of embroidery held in the hand. It is a flood of singing air, water, and sunlight woven into cloth that spirits might wear."

But Hetch Hetchy also had enemies. The rapidly growing city of San Francisco needed a constantly expanding water supply. In 1890, while Congress was debating the bill to create Yosemite National Park, a U.S. Geological Survey engineer reported that Hetch Hetchy Valley would be a fine place to build a reservoir. Its floor was level, its granite walls were steep, and its entrance was narrow, so that it could easily be dammed. A dam penning up the Tuolumne River would create a deep lake of pure fresh water where the valley had been.

A second U.S. Geological Survey report in 1899 came to the same conclusions and added a new argument: Because Hetch Hetchy was completely within Yosemite National Park, there would be no need to buy out private landowners, perhaps at great expense. Thus a Hetch Hetchy reservoir would be cheaper to construct than any of the other possible reservoir sites San Francisco was considering.

Of course, the law establishing Yosemite National Park prohibited such use of park territory. But what Congress had done, Congress could undo. In 1900 the mayor of San Francisco decided that his city needed a reservoir at Hetch Hetchy, and later that year a member of the House of Representatives from California introduced a bill authorizing the Secretary of the Interior "to permit the use of rights through . . . the Yosemite . . . for . . . water conduits and for water plants, dams and reservoirs. . . ." Without much discussion Congress approved the bill, and President McKinley signed it in February, 1901. San Francisco then applied for permission to build a dam at Hetch Hetchy under the terms of the new law.

But by this time Theodore Roosevelt was President, and his tough-minded Secretary of the Interior, Ethan Allen Hitchcock, would not hear of such a desecration of parkland. Three times between 1903 and 1906 he denied the request, and after the third attempt San Francisco decided to look elsewhere for water. In April, 1906, though, the city was struck by an earthquake and a fire. The devastation wrought by the fire made San Francisco's shortage of reliable water supplies all the more obvious, and the demand for a Hetch Hetchy reservoir was revived. Gifford Pinchot, then head of the U.S. Forest Service, declared, "I hope sincerely that in the regeneration of San Francisco its people may be able to make provision for a water supply from the Yosemite National Park. . . . I will stand ready to render any assistance which lies in my power." And Pinchot did render assistance, though it seems an odd thing for a supposed conservationist to have done. He prevailed on the Attorney General to rule that it would be legal for the Secretary of the Interior to grant a license for a dam in a national park. About this time Secretary of the Interior Hitchcock resigned, and the new Secretary, James R. Garfield, a friend of Pinchot's, let it be known that he would look favorably upon the Hetch Hetchy project.

Muir, naturally, had been strongly opposed to the

idea from the moment he heard of it. But he saw no serious threat to Hetch Hetchy so long as Hitchcock held office. In the spring of 1908, however, with San Francisco's application under consideration by Secretary Garfield, Muir wrote to his friend President Roosevelt urging rejection of the Hetch Hetchy proposal: "This valley . . . is one of the most sublime and beautiful and important features of the Park, and to dam and submerge it would be hardly less destructive and deplorable in its effect on the Park in general than would be the damming of Yosemite itself. . . . I am heartily in favor of a Sierra or even a Tuolumne water supply for San Francisco, but all the water required can be obtained from sources outside the Park, leaving the twin valleys, Hetch Hetchy and Yosemite, to the use they were intended for when the Park was established." Roosevelt, who had not paid close attention to the Hetch Hetchy dispute, passed Muir's letter along to Garfield with the suggestion that he take no action on the proposal at present. Roosevelt did think the Secretary might grant San Francisco a license for a reservoir at another site of less scenic value that had also been sought—Lake Eleanor, in the northwest corner of Yosemite National Park. "Why not allow Lake Eleanor, and stop there?" the President asked.

But Garfield had already made up his mind. On May 11, 1908, he signed an order giving *both* Hetch Hetchy and Lake Eleanor to San Francisco. The only concession he made to the conservationists was to ask that the Lake Eleanor site be developed first.

Muir, weary and weak from bronchial colds and savage headaches, found this a devastating blow. But he managed to write consolingly to his Sierra Club associate William Colby, "Never mind, dear Colby, the present flourishing triumphant growth of the wealthy wicked . . . will not thrive forever. . . . We may lose this particular fight, but truth and right must prevail at last. . . ."

There was still hope of saving Hetch Hetchy. First the city of San Francisco had to vote to accept the gift, and then Congress had to give its approval. Muir readied himself for the fight. To his dismay he found the Sierra Club divided: A strong minority of members, living in San Francisco, was ready to sacrifice Hetch Hetchy to the city's needs. Unable to use the Sierra Club as their rallying place, Muir and Colby set up a new organization, the Society for the Preservation of National Parks, with the same address and much the same officers as the Sierra Club. Under its auspices they began distributing material opposing the dam. "A great political miracle this, of 'improving' the beauty of the most beautiful of all mountain parks by cutting down its groves, and burying all the thickets of azalea and wild rose, lily gardens, and ferneries two or three hundred feet deep," Muir wrote. "After this is done we are promised a road blasted on the slope of the north wall, where nature-lovers may sit on rustic stools, or rocks, like frogs on logs, to admire the sham dam lake, the grave of Hetch Hetchy. This Yosemite Park fight began a dozen years ago. Never for a moment have I believed that the American people would fail to defend it for the welfare of themselves and all the world. The people are now aroused. Tidings from far and near show that almost every good man and woman is with us. Therefore be of good cheer, watch, and pray and fight!"

In November, 1908, San Franciscans voted by a margin of 6 to 1 in favor of damming Hetch Hetchy. A month later Congress opened hearings on the proposal. Hundreds of letters opposing the scheme came in, and a long, angry debate began. Muir once more was attacked: A former mayor of San Francisco, testifying in favor of the dam, declared, "He began his career . . . as an operator in a sawmill. Verily 'the lover of the tree destroyeth the tree.'. . . I am sure he would sacrifice his own family for the preservation of beauty. He considers human life very cheap, and he considers the works of God superior. . . ." But these cruel slanders backfired. The Congressional hearings revealed that even the strongest supporters of the dam admitted that many other satisfactory reservoir sites existed in the mountains east of San Francisco. The only advantage the Hetch Hetchy site had was that it would be cheaper, because it was already public land. Cheaper? Who could set a price on Hetch Hetchy? Who could find another such valley, once the reservoir had drowned that one? What did the saving of a few dollars matter, or even the saving of a few million, if a unique place of beauty would be lost for all of time to come? Congress adjourned in March,

1909, without giving its approval to the Hetch Hetchy project. Theodore Roosevelt's term of office expired at the same time, and one of the first acts of his successor, William Howard Taft, was to demand the resignation of Secretary of the Interior Garfield. Hetch Hetchy was safe, for the time being. Robert Underwood Johnson wrote to Muir, "I believe we are going to win!"

Muir diverted himself during these tense months of political maneuvering by taking a number of trips into the mountains. In February, 1909, he revisited the Petrified Forest and then the Grand Canyon in the company of John Burroughs. As usual, Muir set a rugged pace, and the less vigorous Burroughs was hard put to keep up. At the Grand Canyon, a member of their party exclaimed, "To think of our having the Grand Canyon and John Burroughs and John Muir thrown in!" The exhausted Burroughs, with a sour look into the depths of the canyon, muttered, "I wish Muir *was* thrown in, sometimes." But there was no rest for the hapless naturalist. In April Muir took him camping at Yosemite and made him hike the length of the valley. "It was enough to astonish his weary legs," Muir wrote to Helen. "I felt exhilarated and refreshed. Oh, the charm of the mountains!" He was then seventy-one years old.

In October, 1909, President Taft visited Yosemite and invited Muir to be his guide. Here was a fine chance to plead the case for Hetch Hetchy, and Muir quickly accepted. There would be no camping in the mountains, as there had been on Roosevelt's visit, for

Taft was enormously fat and had little love for the outdoor life. But Muir and Taft took short walks on the trails and got along well together. At one point, as they stopped to rest, Taft pointed into Yosemite Valley below and observed that it would make a fine farm. "Why, this is Nature's cathedral, a place to worship in!" Muir cried in alarm, but the President smiled and said, "Don't you think that since these valleys are so far from the centers of population, they might just as well be used commercially? Now that," he said, indicating the entrance to the valley, "would be a fine place for a dam!" Muir began to protest violently—until he realized, by Taft's laughter, that he was only being teased. Taft gave him his word that he would let no harm come to any part of the park, including Hetch Hetchy. A few days later the new Secretary of the Interior, Richard Ballinger, arrived at Yosemite and asked Muir to take him to Hetch Hetchy. After viewing the valley, he declared that he would block any attempt to build a dam there.

Thus Muir had reasons for joy as 1910 opened. Hetch Hetchy was safe; his daughter Helen was in good health and had married a cattle rancher's son at her desert retreat; his other daughter, Wanda, had presented him with his first grandchild. He now spent much of his time with friends in the Los Angeles area, in order to escape the winter fogs of northern California and, perhaps, to get away from the memories haunting the house he had shared with Louie. He was at last able to settle down to work on his books. In 1909 his dog story, *Stickeen,* published in a magazine twelve years earlier, had appeared as a little volume by itself. In the spring of 1910 he unearthed his 1869 journal and made it ready for publication under the title. *My First Summer in the Sierra.* Published in 1911, it is probably his most vivid and exciting book. His next project was an autobiography covering his life up to the time he left the University of Wisconsin to begin his wanderings, called *The Story of My Boyhood and Youth.* Much of the manuscript was finished late in 1910, but he spent so much time revising it that the book did not appear until 1913. At the same time he was working on *The Yosemite,* a guide to the park. Part of it was drawn from his earlier book *The Mountains of California,* but much of the material, including an appeal for the protection of Hetch Hetchy, was new. This book came out in 1912.

He worked so feverishly on all these literary endeavors because he was planning to fulfill in 1911 one of his oldest dreams. "Have I forgotten the Amazon, Earth's greatest river?" he asked a friend early that year. "Never, never, never. It has been burning in me half a century, and will burn forever." In April, 1911, Muir let it be known that he intended to explore the jungles of South America at the age of seventy-three. Those who were close to him pleaded with him to stay home, but he met all protests with the reply, "God will take care of me and bring me home safely."

He went east in June. With Robert Underwood Johnson he visited Washington, saw President Taft and a number of important Senators and

Congressmen, and went away confident that the Hetch Hetchy project would not make a sudden reappearance while he was out of the country. At the end of the month he received an honorary degree at Yale: "I arose with a grand air," he said, "shook my massive academic plumes into finest fluting folds, as became the occasion, stepped forward in awful majesty and stood rigid and solemn like an ancient sequoia while the orator poured praise on the honored wanderer's head." Then he settled in upstate New York for a few weeks to work on the final drafts of *The Story of My Boyhood and Youth* and *The Yosemite.* "I don't know what has got into me, making so many books all at once," he wrote to John Burroughs. "It is not natural. . . ." Muir had invited Burroughs to go with him to the Amazon, but Burroughs, a year older than Muir, thought the idea was insane. "The world's big," Muir replied, "and I want to have a good look at it before it gets dark."

On August 11 he sailed from New York. Three weeks later he was in Brazil and on his way up the Amazon, getting up at four in the morning the day his river journey began so he would miss nothing. By September 5 he was at the rubber-producing city of Manáos, deep in the jungle; there he boarded a steam tug for a side journey up the Amazon's great tributary, the Rio Negro. He went on until dense reeds made it impossible for the tug to continue; then he boarded a skiff, and when the river was too choked even for that, he crept onward on hands and knees through the swamps until the other members of his party made him return. His route next took him back to the coast and southward, and up the Iguassú River into another section of jungle: "Magnificent primeval forest . . . crowns like umbrella tops rising above each other. . . . Tree ferns fifteen to twenty feet high, fronds five feet long. . . ."

In Argentina a few weeks later he found himself a celebrity, surrounded by reporters, scientists, and government officials. He told them he had no plans for writing more books "until I give up my present occupation."

"And what may that be?"

"Tramp," he said. "I'm seventy-four, and still good at it."

He crossed South America by train to Chile, so that he could have a glimpse of the snowy Andes and also so he could search for an almost legendary tree, the twisted, spiky-limbed *Araucaria imbricata,* nicknamed "the monkey-puzzle tree." Only a few explorers had ever seen it, and no one, not even the officials of the Chilean botanical garden, had any clear idea where it might be found. Muir believed the tree grew on the western slopes of the Andes near the snowline, and following his hunch, he went south 500 miles through the mountains, turning inland and ascending them by horseback until he found an entire forest of *Araucaria* on a high ridge. Tentless, he camped overnight in a grove of the bizarre monkey puzzles. "Guess how happy I was and how I stared at and admired these ancient trees," he wrote to Helen.

In December he went back across South America to the port of Montevideo, Uruguay. His South American expedition of three and a half months was over, but he was not going home. Although he had kept it a secret from his friends and family, he had intended all along to continue on to Africa, for there were trees there, too, that he wanted to see. He sailed on December 8, and by the middle of January, 1912, he was in Capetown, South Africa. Northward now he went to awesome Victoria Falls, on the Zambezi River, where his main goal was not the great waterfall itself but the grove of huge baobab trees nearby. "Wandered about in the woods that fringe the Falls, dripping with spray, and through the baobab woods," he wrote to Helen. "It is easily recognized by its skin-like bark, and its massive trunk and branches. The bark . . . looks like leather, or the skin of a hippopotamus. . . . The Falls too are grand and novel. . . . Smoke-like spray ever ascending, watering the woods with constant showers. . . ."

A coastal steamer took him from the port of Beira, in Mozambique, up Africa's eastern coast to Mombasa; then he went inland to visit Lake Victoria and see the source of the Nile; going back to the coast, he headed home by way of the Suez Canal and landed in New York on March 26, tanned and healthy. He stopped there long enough to help John Burroughs celebrate his seventy-fifth birthday, and hurried on home to California to celebrate his own seventy-fourth. From Wanda and Helen he learned that the number of his grandchildren had increased to four in his absence with the birth of Wanda's third son, and Helen soon would have her second.

The journey had been a remarkable one, and deeply gratifying. But it had taken more strength from him than he realized. Almost as soon as he returned he caught a severe cold. He said it came from "breathing the dust in my den"—but his once-powerful body no longer had its old vigor, and recovery was slow, with pneumonia a constant threat. Nevertheless he forced himself to keep on writing. "Just now from every direction grim work is staring me hard in the face . . . and urging concentration and haste," he said. "I'm in my little library den looking over notes, plotting and planning."

He was working now on a book about his adventures in Alaska, and he hoped also to tell the story of his thousand-mile walk to the Gulf of Mexico in 1867 and 1868. But his deep involvement in the conservationist movement demanded much of his time, for the Hetch Hetchy controversy had come back to life.

President Taft had kept the valley safe throughout his term in the White House. San Francisco had repeatedly asked permission to build a dam there, and each time the request had been refused. The last such denial, in November, 1912, bluntly instructed the city to seek elsewhere for its reservoir. But Taft was defeated in the 1912 election, and on March 4, 1913, Woodrow Wilson became President. He chose as his Secretary of the Interior the former city attorney of San Francisco, Franklin K. Lane. A man who had been in charge of the legal aspects of San Francisco's early attempts to get possession of Hetch Hetchy now had the chief voice in determining the valley's fate.

Once more the city asked for the valley. The situation was desperate, but Muir again sent forth a flood of appeals, articles, letters, and statements. Newspapers around the country joined the campaign to save Hetch Hetchy. Wilson, an Easterner who knew little about the problem, left the matter in Secretary Lane's hands. "Our enemies now seem to be having most everything their own wicked way," Muir wrote to the naturalist Henry Fairfield Osborn on July 15, 1913. "Think of three or four ambitious, shifty traders and politicians calling themselves 'The City of San Francisco,' bargaining with the United States for half of the Yosemite Park like Yankee horse-traders. . . ." A bill to give the valley to San Francisco was now making its way through Congress. Muir fought it as hard as he could, but on September 3 it passed in the House of Representatives by a vote of 183 to 43. He could hope now only for its defeat in the Senate. It was a grim time for him. He was lost in bitter loneliness, for most of those who had been closest to him now had gone to their graves—his mother, his brothers and sisters, his wife, Mrs. Carr, William Keith, Harriman, all the friends of early days and late. Now even Hetch Hetchy was slipping from his grasp. On November 15 he wrote to Helen, "The H.H. question will probably be decided in the first week of December next and I still think we will win. Anyhow I'll be relieved when it's settled, for it's killing me." And it was. Anxiety over Hetch Hetchy was draining his vitality. He coughed all the time, and his lungs were weakening.

The Senate passed the Hetch Hetchy bill at midnight on December 6, 43-25. "We still hope the President will veto it," the heartbroken Muir told Helen. "Anyhow I've done my best, and am now free to go on with my pen work. . . . I'm somewhat run down for want of exercise, and exhausting work and worry. . . ." But Wilson signed the bill into law on December 19. Hetch Hetchy was lost.

Muir could not hide his grief. Robert B. Marshall of the U.S. Geological Survey, who visited him at this time, wrote, "It was sorrowful indeed to see him sitting in his cobwebbed study in his lonely house . . . with the full force of his defeat upon him, after the struggle of a lifetime in the service of Hetch Hetchy. It was one of the most pathetic things I ever witnessed, and I could not but think that if Congress, the President, and even the San Francisco contingent could have seen him, they would certainly have been willing to have delayed any action until the old man had gone away—and I fear that is going to be very soon, as he appeared to me to be breaking very fast."

He was spared, at least, from having to see Hetch Hetchy desecrated. Engineering difficulties caused long delays in building the dam and greatly increased its expense; the job took many years, and by then John Muir was at rest. Those who come to Hetch

Hetchy today, and there are not many of them, behold a grisly sight, a murdered valley. A Sierra Club film of 1955, David Brower's *Two Yosemites,* provides some somber views and a dark narration: "What you see here is what you see at most fluctuating reservoirs and what no one should see in a park. Stumps where the basin was cleared, stumps and more stumps, exposed and reexposed until silt finally buries them. The stream—it was one of the most beautiful in the Sierra—is silted in. Tuolumne Falls is covered. The banks are silted. The flat living space is silted, and as soon as the surface is dry enough, it is on the move—a dust bowl, from the silt that sloughed off the canyonsides when the reservoir was full. The river brings still more each year, and wind-blown scum collects in the eddies of what was a sparkling river." The destruction of Hetch Hetchy cost $100,000,000; modern water experts agree that San Francisco's needs could have been met without touching the valley at all.

Muir, always the optimist, managed to declare that "some compensating good must surely follow" from the death of Hetch Hetchy, and in this he was right. Having sacrificed one valley, Congress made amends of sort in 1916 by passing a bill creating a National Park Service to watch over the parks and imposing strong new regulations to prevent further impairment of their natural resources. The sponsor of this bill was Representative William Kent of California, who in 1908 had given the nation the grove of redwood trees near San Francisco that became Muir Woods National Monument. A Sierra Club man, Stephen T. Mather, became the first director of the National Park Service. Thereafter it became much more difficult to invade the sanctity of the parks—although in the 1960's the Sierra Club had to work hard to defeat a proposal that would have built dams in the Grand Canyon.

Though he spoke of the Hetch Hetchy episode as "a monumental crime," Muir tried to put the tragedy behind him and return to the writing of *Travels in Alaska*. Through the early months of 1914 he worked as hard as his failing strength would permit, interrupting his toil only for visits to his daughters and grandchildren. He had suffered a terrible blow in his old age, but Hetch Hetchy aside, he could look back in tranquillity and pleasure at a long and happy life. His boyhood in Scotland, his hard years on his father's farm, his university days, his cunning mechanical inventions, his early wanderings in Canada and Florida, his wondrous discovery of the beauty of the Sierra Nevada, his Yosemite years, his valuable research on glaciers, his Alaskan adventures, his glacial scramble with Stickeen, his career as a writer and as a crusader for the protection of the wilderness, his role in creating and preserving the national parks, his successful marriage and rewarding children—all these things were compensations enough for the final sadness of losing Hetch Hetchy. And he hoped he had a few books left in him, and perhaps a few adventures, too.

But the shadows deepened. In the summer of 1914

war broke out in Europe. He had hated war all his life, and now he spoke of the German invasion of Belgium as something "monstrous" and "horrible." He contributed funds for the relief of war victims, but news of the slaughter left him shaken and depressed.

On September 1, 1914, there took place a smaller event, but one that had great symbolic impact for John Muir. The last passenger pigeon in existence, a slender gray-and-brown bird named Martha, died in the Cincinnati Zoo at the age of twenty-nine. As a boy, Muir had read Audubon's account of the "immense legions" of these pigeons he had seen over Kentucky, so many that "the noonday light was obscured as by an eclipse." A few years later Muir himself had stared in wonder at the pigeons, uncountable multitudes of them darkening the Wisconsin sky. But now they were gone in all their billions. Man had hunted them and hunted them all through the nineteenth century, and he had driven them from the world with his guns, bombarding them into extinction. The passenger pigeon would never be seen on earth again, and now John Muir began to think of taking his own leave of a world where greed and cruelty and stupidity too often triumphed over beauty and innocence. In the fall of 1914 he began refurbishing his house, even installing electricity—not for himself, but to get it ready for whichever of his daughters cared to live in it when he was gone. He wrote to Wanda to tell her he wished to be buried on the ranch, next to his wife. In December, he said he wanted to visit Helen and her family at her Mojave Desert home, and Wanda came to help him get ready. They both knew it would be his last journey.

He closed up the Alhambra Valley house, leaving behind his books, his collections, his clocks and other youthful inventions. They all are still there, too, for the John Muir House has become a national historical site, and the National Park Service maintains it as it was when he lived there. Carrying the nearly completed manuscript of *Travels in Alaska,* he set out by train for the desert. He reached the town where Helen lived at half past two in the morning, with a chill wind blowing, and he began to shiver during the automobile ride to her house. But in the morning he brightened in the dry heat of the desert and went out with Helen for a walk, strolling about a mile and pausing often to examine the plants sprouting in the sands. He worked on his book that evening, but he felt faint as he stood up and had to be carried to bed. A doctor was summoned, found that he had pneumonia, and ordered him taken to a hospital in Los Angeles.

Resting there, with Wanda visiting him constantly, he seemed to regain his strength; his natural good humor returned, and he talked of working and traveling again. Death held no perils for him and never had, but he felt there still were things for him to do and see. He was not to have the opportunity. On Christmas Eve, 1914, death came for him. He was alone, as he had been for so many of his other adventures. His nurse had stepped briefly out of his room, and when she went back to him, a moment later, she found him lying as if asleep, for the mountains and glaciers had called his spirit home to them.

Bibliography

BADÊ, WILLIAM FREDERIC, *The Life and Letters of John Muir.* Boston, Houghton Mifflin, 1924.

BROWER, DAVID, ed., *Gentle Wilderness: The Sierra Nevada.* San Francisco, The Sierra Club, 1967.

GUNSKY, FREDERIC R., ed., *South of Yosemite: Selected Writings by John Muir.* Garden City, New York, The Natural History Press, 1968.

JONES, HOLWAY R., *John Muir and the Sierra Club: The Battle for Yosemite.* San Francisco, The Sierra Club, 1965.

MUIR, JOHN, *Cruise of the Corwin.* Boston, Houghton Mifflin, 1918.

———, *The Mountains of California.* New York, The Century Company, 1894.

———, *My First Summer in the Sierra.* Boston, Houghton Mifflin, 1911.

———, *Our National Parks.* Boston, Houghton Mifflin, 1901.

———, *Steep Trails.* Boston, Houghton Mifflin, 1918.

———, *Stickeen.* Boston, Houghton Mifflin, 1909.
———, *The Story of My Boyhood and Youth.* Boston, Houghton Mifflin, 1913.
———, *A Thousand-Mile Walk to the Gulf.* Boston, Houghton Mifflin, 1917.
———, *Travels in Alaska.* Boston, Houghton Mifflin, 1915.
———, *The Yosemite.* New York, The Century Company, 1912.
SILVERBERG, ROBERT, *Vanishing Giants: The Story of the Sequoias.* New York, Simon & Schuster, 1969.
SMITH, HERBERT F., *John Muir.* New York, Twayne Publishers, 1965.
TEALE, EDWIN WAY, ed., *The Wilderness World of John Muir.* Boston, Houghton Mifflin, 1954.
TILDEN, FREEMAN, *The National Parks.* New York, Alfred A. Knopf, 1951.
WOLFE, LINNIE MARSH, *Son of the Wilderness: The Life of John Muir.* New York, Alfred A. Knopf, 1945.

Index

The Author

Robert Silverberg has been a full-time free-lance author based in New York since his graduation from Columbia University in 1956. He has published dozens of books and hundreds of articles. Among his popular books from Putnam's are *The Dawn of Medicine, Men Who Mastered the Atom,* and *Four Men Who Changed the Universe.*

Silverberg, Robert

John Muir, prophet among the glaciers

DATE DUE

JAN 2 1975			
JUN 2 1976			
FEB 3 1977			
OCT 1 1981			
NOV 8 1988			